The Insider's Guide to
Living Like a Local in Italy

Suzanne Pidduck
Founder of Rentvillas.com

Copyright Suzanne Pidduck, 2007
ISBN 978-1-4357-0518-0

INTRODUCTION

Use this guide to enhance your rental experience!

Guidebooks are helpful, but most fall short of the "guidance" you need for renting your own property. Why? Because living like a native is nothing like staying in a hotel! Whether you're packing for your adventure or trying to figure out how to grocery shop in another language, staying in your own home-away-from-home presents a different set of challenges.

Over the years I've made many trips to Italy: first as a student, then a single traveler, later as a mother of three, and finally as the owner of Rentvillas.com. Part how-to, part insider's guide, this traveler's companion is based on my experiences as a renter. You'll find dining suggestions and recommendations for must-see sights as well as all the nuts and bolts of traveling to Italy, such as airport arrivals and surviving on the road. If I've overlooked something, please drop me a line and help me add to these words of wisdom!

Buon viaggio!

Suzanne Pidduck
Rentvillas.com Founder
(800) 726-6702
www.rentvillas.com

CONTENTS

Introduction 1

Before You Leave Home 5
    What to do from the time your trip is confirmed until the day you get on the plane.

Arriving In Italy 19
    Flying into Rome, Milan, Pisa, Florence, or Venice; using the train or bus; driving.

En Route to Your Property 31
    Getting cash, calling your key holder, picking up groceries and basic supplies, Italian cuisine, and recipes.

Making the Most of Your Stay 41
    Meeting your key holder, etiquette and attitude, bugs and deterrents, keeping the house warm/cool, utilities,
and basics of Italian life.

Cities of Italy 53
    Rome, Florence, and Venice.

Regions of Italy 71
    Tuscany, Umbria, Cinque Terre, Italian Lakes, Veneto, Amalfi Coast, and Sicily.

Useful Vocabulary 114

Metric Conversions 115

Index 116

CHAPTER ONE:
BEFORE YOU LEAVE HOME

Even after booking your rental, a good deal of planning is needed to make your trip a success. Don't miss any essential details! Read this section to find out what you need to do...

...After your trip is confirmed

...Three months prior to departure

...One month prior to departure

...Two weeks prior to departure

At the end of this section you will also find a **packing checklist** listing all the handy little items any villa renter might need.

AFTER YOUR TRIP IS CONFIRMED:

Travel Insurance: When you're investing this much in a trip, you want to ensure that you're protected if anything goes wrong. That's why we recommend taking out travel insurance. It's not often needed-- but when it is, boy does it help! A dependable company we often recommend is CSA Travel Protection, found at www.csatravelprotection.com

Cooks, Tours, and Extra Services: If you're thinking of arranging any special services during your stay, the time to do it is now! Cooks are often booked months in advance, so if you'd like a meal prepared the night you arrive you should make arrangements ASAP. Here are a few helpful links to various services in Italy:

- **Cook Service:** For cook services anywhere within Italy, the best company by far is Tasty Italy. This agency networks chefs across the country to reach your villa, wherever you are. www.tastyitaly.com

- **Tuscan Cook Service:** For clients in Tuscany we often recommend Bob the Cook. Do reserve him as early as possible... after all, he's only one man! www.bobthecook.com

- **Special Cook Service:** Located in the Chianti, Matisse will go anywhere and do anything to realize your perfectly envisioned event. He can arrange single meals or orchestrate a "cullinary weekend" with classes. www.chiantichef.com

- **Self-Guided Tours:** Guiding your own tours might seem a little strange... but what it really means is that you get to go on trips that you select and complete at your own pace, on the days you choose. It's like having your own personal guidebook, complete with driving directions from (and back to) your front door. Italia Roadrunners has a selection of itineraries for most of our villa locations. Contact David Wagner at ItaliaRoadrunners@comcast.net or call 1-888-277-4754.

- **Walking Tours:** Context Travel offers a really unique way to see Florence, Rome, or Naples. Walk through the city with an architect, historian, or art expert to see these cities in a whole new way. www.contexttravel.com

- **Italian Tours:** La Dolce Vita is the way to tour in style. Your private tour guide is also your driver! Tours are offered in every region. www.ladolcevitatours.com

- **More Italian Tours:** One Step Closer offers culture, food, wine, sports, and kid-friendly tours around Florence, Tuscany, and Rome. www.onestepcloser.net

- **Golf:** To book any golf course in Italy, go to www.golfy.com.

- **Traveling With Kids:** To get some ideas for activities and sights that your children will enjoy, visit www.travelforkids.com before you leave.

- **Museum Reservations:** You will be *very* happy if you make reservations for the major museums prior to your departure! Nothing is worse than standing in long lines for hours. To book ahead, visit one of the following sites:

   www.tickitaly.it

   www.rome-museum.com

   www.florenceart.it

For more activities specific to the region where you'll be staying, check Chapter Five (Cities of Italy) and Chapter Six (Regions of Italy).

THREE MONTHS PRIOR TO DEPARTURE:

Documents: It's a good idea to make copies of all your travel documents before you leave. Pack the copies separate from the originals. Make a travel itinerary, complete with flight numbers, addresses, and phone numbers; take one copy with you and leave another at home with someone who can be contacted easily.

- **Passport:** Needless to say, you must have your passports with you. Make sure they won't expire during your trip. Having extra passport photos with you can also save vacation time. No visa is necessary for visits of 90 days or less.

- **Other Necessities:** If you wear glasses, bring an extra pair. Likewise, bring your medical insurance ID card and a claim form. If you'll be driving, consider getting an International Driving Permit from any AAA office. While not required, the permit can help if you encounter an Italian policeman who doesn't speak English. To get the permit, you need two passport photos and a U.S. driver's license.

- **Rental Voucher:** Watch the mail a few weeks before your departure for your voucher. This envelope includes the **local name** (probably different from our unique name) and address of your property and any directions needed for getting there. You will need to show this document to the key holder when you arrive, so don't leave it behind!

Arrange for Car Rental: If you're staying in a city like Florence or Rome, you will not need or want to rent a car. However, if you're staying outside of a city, you'll definitely need one! All major rental companies are represented in Italy. You must be at least 21 to rent a car. Insurance policies vary, so be sure to check your policy before you leave home. For the lowest rates and the best selection, we recommend Autoeurope (www.autoeurope.com). If you'll be renting for more than 17 days, consider leasing a car instead. Renault Eurodrive (www.eurodrive.renault.com) specializes in this service, and Autoeurope also offers the option. Also consider choosing a car with GPS (or taking one with you) to avoid getting lost. When you pick up your rental car, make sure to ask whether it takes diesel or not (if possible, request diesel when you reserve the car; it's a much better value in Italy).

CAR RENTAL DISCOUNT:

So many of our clients use Autoeurope that they've decided to give Rentvillas.com customers a 10% discount! Here's how to get it:
- Call **1-800-730-8036**
- At the **beginning of your conversation**, state clearly that you are a Rentvillas client.
- Give the service representative the following discount code: **12-008103**

Please note that our discount cannot be combined with any other special offers that are in effect.

Car Insurance: It is virtually impossible to decline paying for the CDW (collision damage waiver) when renting a car in Italy. Many rental providers insist that you purchase CDW, and most credit card companies will not provide coverage for cars rented in Italy. In addition, there is now an obligatory theft protection fee as well as a 12% airport pick-up charge. One way to avoid some of these extra fees is to rent your car in another country and drive it into Italy. However, you *must* check with the car rental company (and the credit card company if you plan to use your card to cover the CDW) about driving the car into Italy. In addition, find out about any drop-off charges. There is also usually an extra charge for additional drivers. Again, Autoeurope's all inclusive rates are very competitive.

ONE MONTH PRIOR TO DEPARTURE:

Cell Phones: Because of widespread use of cell phones in Europe, many property owners are pulling out their land lines. So be aware that your rental may not have a phone unless specifically stated in the description. Cell phones are also convenient for communicating on-the-go or calling ahead for directions if you get lost on the way! You may want to consider obtaining a cell phone to use while in Italy. Here's how:

- Ask your phone company if your cell phone is a GSM that can be "unlocked" for widespread use. You can then purchase a prepaid cell phone SIM card: a small chip that inserts into your phone. Cellular Abroad (www.cellularabroad.com) will ship your SIM card to you before you leave. Within Italy, look for the name TIM or Vodafone; both are large cellular service providers. Minutes can be added to the SIM card at a gas station or tabaccao. Ask for a *carta di ricarica*, payable in Euros.

- If you don't have a GSM phone, you can purchase an inexpensive GSM phone from TIM or Vodafone in Italy. You can also rent one from Cellular Abroad before you leave.

Laptop & Internet Options: If you'll be taking your laptop with you on the trip, this is the time to make sure you have everything you need to function. The current in Italy is 220-240 volts (110 in the US), so ensure that your laptop can handle the change. If not, you'll need a current converter, which can be purchased at Magellan's (www.magellans.com). You will probably also need a European plug adaptor. If your rental has a phone line, you will need to bring a phone cord to plug into the wall. Remember to check with your ISP to see if they provide a dial-up number in your area (if not, try AOL or Earthlink). Net-roamer, another software application, enables you to access local service providers at the cost of a local call. For more information, visit www.net-roamer.com.

A simpler way to get connected is to go wireless. You can purchase a European compatible wireless card at www.sierrawireless.com/product/ac850.aspx.

If you won't be bringing your laptop, you can still access the internet from one of the many cyber-cafés scattered across the country. You can find a listing of cafés in Italy on **www.cybercafes.com**. A popular internet point chain is Internet Train: **www.internettrain.it**.

Travel Supplies: For travel supplies of every kind, from travel pillows to luggage to all manner of computer and phone related adaptors, we recommend Magellan's (**www.magellans.com**). For a free catalog, call (800) 962-4943.

TWO WEEKS PRIOR TO DEPARTURE:

Rental Voucher: You should have received this document in the mail by now. Your rental voucher includes the **local name** (which will probably be different from our unique name) and address of your property and any directions needed for getting there. You will need to show this document to the key holder when you arrive, so don't leave it behind! Pack it with your other important documents and make a copy to carry separately. You may want to try locating your property on www.viamichelin.com. Please note that some countryside locations may not have an exact "street address." The directions may seem a little confusing when you first read them. However, the road system in Italy is different than it is the US, and it is likely that the directions will make sense once you are on the road. But if you *do* get lost, don't panic! You can always stop and call the contact listed on your voucher.

Money: You may want to have some foreign currency on hand before you depart; it will come in handy for those initial bus, train, or taxi fares, as well as for the security deposit at your property (most require cash upon arrival). To purchase Euros before leaving the U.S., check with your bank. To compare rates, you can also visit www.ordercurrency.com or www.purchasecurrency.com. These websites allow you to pay for the currency by check or credit card, and it will be delivered to you within 48 hours. Another option is changing money at the airport upon your arrival in Italy. Don't depend on withdrawing all of the money you need from an ATM when you arrive, as most ATMs (and bank cards) have daily withdrawal limits. If you'll be using a credit card or a bank card in Italy, call your bank and let them know when you'll be traveling. For security, most banks and credit card companies will lock a card if they suddenly see a purchase in another country.

Weather Considerations: If you pack sensibly and read up on the seasonal climate shifts in the regions you plan to visit, Italy won't deliver any major weather surprises. Thanks to the moderating influence of the sea and the protective barrier of the Alps, Italy enjoys a temperate climate. There is, however, a lot of variation depending on where you are. In winter, the Alps are very cold and both the Po Valley and central Appenines are swathed in pea soup fog. The coastlines of Liguria,

Campania, and Sicilia are mild in the winter and hot in the summer. Spring and autumn are ideal for tramping through museums and the like, while winter and summer are great times for going to the mountains. Beware of beaches in August, when everyone and their grandmother heads to the seaside. Better months for beach bathing are June, July, and September. Major cities are also less desireable in August: shops are closed, it's hot, and you'll find yourself surrounded by more tourists than Italians. So, while it is impossible to predict the weather conditions, it's safe to assume that July and August will be quite warm and humid. May, June, September, and October are generally mild. During April and October there can be rain and chilly temperatures in the evening, so be prepared. A lightweight raincoat and silk long underwear are easy to pack and take up very little space. You may never need them, but on the other hand you may be very happy you brought them along! Of course, it's smart to review the local weather forecast before leaving. For the best information on weather in Italy, visit **www.weather.com**.

PACKING CHECKLIST:

After twenty-odd years of renting properties in Europe, we've compiled the following list of useful items to bring along (please note that many of these items will need to go in your checked luggage):

- ☐ Plastic cutting board and serrated knife
- ☐ Pocket knife with screwdriver and corkscrew
- ☐ Kitchen/scrub sponge (cheaper and more durable in the US)
- ☐ Baggies and zip-lock bags in various sizes
- ☐ Rubber bands and twist ties
- ☐ Matches
- ☐ Salt and pepper
- ☐ Spices in zip-lock bags
- ☐ Extra batteries for cameras, etc.
- ☐ Small flashlight
- ☐ Emergency TP or tissue pack
- ☐ Small pack of hand wipes or baby wipes
- ☐ 1-2 bars of bath soap
- ☐ Washcloths (not usually available in France)
- ☐ Powdered detergent in zip-lock bag
- ☐ Laundry stain stick for spots
- ☐ Travel alarm clock
- ☐ Pocket calculator (for currency conversion)
- ☐ Personal music player with small speakers
- ☐ String bag or "pocket" backpack for shopping

- ☐ Ear plugs - you never know!
- ☐ Money belt or pouch
- ☐ Paperback Italian cookbook
- ☐ For kids: Powdered drink mix to stir into regular or fizzy water certainly beats the cost of bottled drinks, and it's easy to transport!
- ☐ Small portable book light
- ☐ Old pillowcase in case of scratchy bed linen or to store dirty clothes on the trip home.
- ☐ Comfortable walking shoes
- ☐ Old pool towels (you can leave behind)
- ☐ Small umbrella - regardless of the season
- ☐ Slippers or flip-flops - for cold floors
- ☐ Insect repellant (see "Mosquitoes, Screens, and Deterrents," Chapter Four)
- ☐ A GSM-compatible cell phone - your own or rented
- ☐ A pocket English-Italian dictionary

CHAPTER TWO:
ARRIVING IN ITALY

Now that you've booked your property and (hopefully!) a flight into Italy, it's time to think about how you'll get from the airport to your property. Check out this section to find information about what to do if you're...

…Flying into Rome

…Flying into Milan/Malpensa

…Flying into Pisa, Florence, or Venice

…Taking the train or bus

At the end of this chapter you will also find a section about **driving in Italy**. Brush up on this chapter before getting into your rental car!

FLYING INTO ROME:

There are two airports in Rome: Fiumicino (also called Leonardo da Vinci) and Ciampino. Most international flights arrive in Fiumicino, about an hour west of Rome. There are a variety of ways to get in and out of the city.

- **Shuttle and Transfer Services:** This is probably the best option for getting into the city, and it is certainly the most comfortable after a long flight. Here are some companies to contact online:

    www.romeshuttlelimousine.com

    http://rome.airports-shuttle.com

    www.rome-airport-shuttle.com

- **Taxi:** Oddly, this option can be more expensive than a shuttle/transfer service. Make sure to take an officially marked taxi: white with a "taxi" light on top and a license number. To reserve a taxi in advance or if you have special needs, go to www.3570.it. You can also call a cab by dialing (+39) 06 3570.

- **Train:** You can take the Leonardo Express directly into Rome's main station, Stazione Termini, and then hop into a cab or bus to your final destination. Buy your tickets at the airport train ticket counter or from a vending machine, and then follow the signs with the train symbol. Be sure to validate your ticket in the machines on the platform before you enter the train. A nonstop service leaves about every 30 minutes for Termini Station, running from 6:30 AM to 11:30 PM.

- **Rental Cars:** Various agencies can be reached by following the signs for *autonoleggio* (car rental) down a long passageway. If you'll be overnighting in Rome, consider picking up a rental car in the city rather than at the airport; it's easier and avoids the airport pickup charge. For information about reserving a rental car in advance, see Chapter One.

- **Airport Hotel:** If you have an early flight out of Rome, we recommend staying at the Hilton Hotel, located right at the Fiumicino airport. At www.hilton.com, enter Rome and Italy. You will find two Hiltons listed in Rome; the one you want is the Hilton Rome Airport Hotel.

- **Driving North:** To head north along the west coast, take the A12 autostrada. When it ends north of Civitavecchia, continue along the coast on the SS1 Aurelia. To hook up with the Autostrada del Sole (connecting Rome with Florence and Milan), follow the signs for the A1.

FLYING INTO MILAN/MALPENSA:

The Milano-Malpensa airport is actually about 50 kilometers northwest of the city of Milan. If you're catching a train from Milan to another city, you will likely need to get to Milano Centrale Station. There are several options for getting into Milan:

- **Taxi:** Metered taxis are available outside the Arrival Terminal. The trip time into the city should be about 50 minutes, depending upon traffic.

- **Train:** The Malpensa Express departs from Terminal 1 on the lower ground floor about every 30 minutes. It terminates at the Cadorna Railway Station and runs from 6:45 AM to 9:45 PM. To reach the Milano Centrale station (where most other trains depart), you will need to take a cab.

- **Shuttle Bus:** Outside Terminal 1 you can catch a shuttle bus that will take you directly to Milano Centrale station. Shuttles leave from 6:20 AM to about midnight and take about an hour. From Milano Centrale it is easy to catch a train to other destinations.

- **Hotel:** Hotel Villa Malpensa is nearest the airport. Website: **www.hotelvillamalpensa.com**. First Hotel is about ten minutes away but provides a shuttle bus. Website: **www.firsthotel.it**

- **Overnight in Parma:** Should you decide to head south before finding a hotel, consider stopping in Parma, about two hours south of Malpensa. It's an elegant and sophisticated city, often overlooked by tourists. Parmigiano cheese and prosciutto both originated in Parma. If you have time to explore the city, don't miss the beautiful baptistry located next to the Duomo. Pink and octagonal, it is affectionately referred to as *Il Porcellino*, or "the little pig." The Jolly Hotel Parma is very nice and excellently located in the center of town. (Via Bodoni 3, Tel. (+39) 0521 208057)

FLYING INTO OTHER AIRPORTS:

Pisa Arrival: Flying into Pisa's Galileo Galilei Airport is very convenient. Several airlines fly into Pisa, including British Airways, Air France, Lufthansa, and Alitalia. Delta Airlines also has flights from New York to Pisa. From the airport, you can take the local train (about a hundred yards away) into Pisa Centrale station, and then to Florence or other destinations. Train tickets can be purchased at the information office in the Arrival Terminal. It is also very easy to arrange for the pick-up of a rental car.

Florence Arrival: Amerigo Vespucci Airport (La Peretola), just outside Florence, has become popular for arrivals. It has convenient flights between several European cities, including London, Paris, and Brussels. The terminal includes a restaurant, bank, and car rentals. The process of arrival, going through customs, and taxiing into the center of Florence is usually a breeze.

Venice Arrival: Many major European airlines use Marco Polo Airport. It's located on the mainland, a thirty-minute water taxi ride away from the city. There are also less expensive methods for reaching Venice. Water busses take about an hour, while blue ATVO busses will take you to Piazzale Roma, where you can catch a *vaporetto* (the least expensive option). If you need to stay near the airport for a night, try. **www.venicerestor.it**.

TAKING THE TRAIN:

Italy's system of trains can be a quick and convenient way to get from place to place. You may need to take the train on the way to your property, or you may want to use the train to take a day trip during your stay. Train schedules and information can be found at www.raileurope.com.

It's definitely worthwhile to buy tickets in advance for any long trip, particularly in the busy seasons. In general, there is a base charge for the ticket itself, and then an optional charge for a seat reservation (available only on some trains). Advance booking is required on the Pendolino, the high-speed train, and on some of the inter-city (IC) trains.

If you'll be using the train for three days or more during your trip, consider buying a Trenitalia Pass, which you can use as many times as you want for three days during a given sixty-day period. (You can also add on travel days if you need more.) This pass acts like an unlimited ticket, but any seat reservations you make will still be at an extra cost.

For questions about schedules and rates while at the train station, go to the *informazioni* counter, marked with a capital "I."

TAKING THE BUS:

Most bus headquarters are located at or near the train station. In big cities, schedules for the buses are (usually) available and can be useful for mapping your routes. If that fails, try asking a local. Pay close attention to bus numbers, as some have letters appended. For example, bus 25A is not the same as bus 25.

Bus tickets can be purchased at a *tabacchi*, a newspaper kiosk, ticket machines near main stops, or from many bars. Tickets are valid for a specific duration of time (60 minutes, for example), regardless of destination. If you don't know how long it will take to get from one place to another, ask.

Once on the bus, you will need to validate your ticket using the ticket box, usually mounted to a post in the bus. The ticket is now "live" and you will need to get off before the time stated on the ticket expires, or validate another ticket.

When exiting the bus, it is polite to stand up and move to the doors a short time before the bus halts at your stop, so that you will be ready to get off. If there is a button to push to tell the driver to stop, do so. If you aren't sure how far away your stop is, tell the driver when you get on and he will notify you at the appropriate time.

DRIVING IN ITALY:

Driving in Italy is about the same as driving in any other European country... hair-raising at best! You may be on the road for the first time abroad, so stay alert and be courteous to other drivers. We've assembled some pointers specifically for driving in Italy:

- **Navigation:** Cars do drive on the right, but you'll discover the Italian road system is different than the U.S. The best way to get where you're going is to start with a good map and a driving companion. Know the name of the towns along your route. Follow the signs to the first town, and then to the next, and so on, until you reach your destination.

- **Speed Limits:**
  Highway: 130 km/h
  Major Roads: 90 km/h
  Towns: 50 km/h.

- **Left Lane:** Reserved for passing. *Divieto di sorpasso a destra* means "no passing on the right." Expect other cars to flash their lights and honk if you don't observe this rule.

- **Low-Beam Lights:** Must be turned on whenever you are driving.

- **Cell Phones:** Use with a headset if driving.

- **Roundabouts:** You will find some roundabouts in Italy. They are very practical and quite convenient once you get the hang of them; if you miss an exit, just go around again! Note that incoming traffic does *not* have the right-of-way.

- **City Driving:** Don't try it! Most of the historical centers have ZTL signs posted: *Zona Traffico Limitato* (Limited Traffic Zone). This means that unless you have a special sticker given to residents of the city, you are not even allowed to drive through, let alone park your car! Driving in smaller towns is much easier. (Just look out for pedestrian areas.)

- **Tolls:** Be prepared for the pay tolls located along the *autostrade*. Have a supply of at least 25 Euros in cash before leaving the airport to pay the tolls, which can be expensive. Chances are that you can also use a credit card. At some toll booths you must pay a set amount immediately; at others you push a button to receive a ticket and pay when exiting the toll road. A Via-Card (pre-paid toll card) can be purchased at the autogrills or at the *autostrade* toll booths.

• **Buying Gas:** Most gas stations accept credit cards, but it's wise to keep cash on hand. If you want to fill the tank, say, "*Mi faccia il pieno, per favore.*" Most gas stations are only full service, and they will check the oil and wash the windows if you ask. "*Puo controllare l'olio?*" means "Can you check the oil?" Some other useful terms are *benzina* (gasoline), *gasolio* (diesel), *benzina verde* (unleaded), and *SP* or *senza piombo* (unleaded). Make sure you know what kind of gasoline your rental car uses. Most likely it will be diesel, which is less expensive that gasoline. Also, there are no gas stations in the center of Florence. Always fill up in the outskirts.

• **Food Stops:** There are several *autogrills* (large restaurants) located just off the Autostrada A1. They accept credit cards. Service is cafeteria style, but the selection is broad and the food is generally-good. (Note: When stopping for a drink at the bar, pay for your drink and then submit your receipt to the *barista*. When you present the receipt at the bar your order will be filled.) When exiting at most of these *autostrada* restaurant stops you will be forced to walk through a deli/gift shop first. They sell everything from toys to prosciutto and pastries.

• **Helpful Phrases:**
  ♦ *Entrata* - Entrance
  ♦ *Uscita* - Exit
  ♦ *Senso Unico* - One-Way
  ♦ *Strada Senza Uscita* - Dead-End Street
  ♦ *Strada Deformata* - Street Under Repair
  ♦ *Rallentare* - Slow Down
  ♦ *Divieto di Sosta* - No Parking
  ♦ *Zona Pedonale* - Pedestrian Zone
  ♦ *Passo Carrabile* - Don't Block Driveway
  ♦ *Caduta Massi* - Beware Falling Rocks
  ♦ *Nebbia* - Fog

- **Street Signs By Color:**
  ♦ Yellow or Brown - Hotels, restaurants, museums, and other points of interest.
  ♦ White - Train stations (*stazione*), town center, etc. The symbol for the town center (*centro*) is concentric black circles on a white background.
  ♦ Blue and Green - Directional road signs. The green signs are for the *autostrade*. While on the *autostrade*, you will see small signs in the median divider, giving the distance to exits ahead. You will very seldom see a listing of cities and corresponding distances as would be found in the U.S. The small signs will also advise you of the distance to the next *area di servizio*, or gas station. Round blue signs with the letter "P" in the center mean parking! These are very imporant to look for, since finding a place to park is always difficult in Italian towns and cities.
  ♦ Blue and White - Tourist information offices, found in most small towns, are marked with a white "i" on a circular blue background.

Arriving in Italy • 29

INTERNATIONAL ROAD SIGNS:

 No Entry

 Yield

 Informational Sign (a bumpy road)

 Closed to All Vehicles

 Closed to Cars

 No Parking (red & blue)

 Speed Limit in Kilometers

CHAPTER THREE:
EN ROUTE TO YOUR PROPERTY

After you've arranged to get to your property, what should you do just prior to showing up at the front door? Check this section out for tips on...

...Getting cash

...Calling your key holder

...Picking up basic supplies

...Grocery shopping (with shopping list)

At the end of this chapter you will also find a section about **Italian cuisine**. Consult this section for some easy Italian recipes or brush up on vocabulary before going out to eat. *Buon appetito!*

CASH:

If you don't have Euros with you, now is the time to get some at the airport. Exchange U.S. Currency at a money changing window or withdraw cash from an ATM, or *Bancomat*. Be aware that ATM machines or your card often have a daily withdrawal limit.

CALLING YOUR KEY HOLDER:

Many key holders will request that you call in advance of your arrival so that they don't have to wait at the property for several hours. One of the many advantages to having a GSM cell phone (see Chapter One) with you is that you can easily call the key holder to advise them of any change in your arrival time.

If you need to make a call from a public phone at the airport, coin-operated public telephones are no longer used. You will need to buy a telephone card at a post office, tobacco shop (*tabacchi*), train station, or newspaper stand. In Italy, phone numbers can be anywhere from 4 to 8 digits. Land lines start with a 0, while most cell phone numbers begin with 3. To reach other countries from within Italy, dial 0, the country code, and then the phone number. Italy's country code is 39. Example: The phone number for the U.S. Embassy in Rome is 06 4674 2244 from within Italy and (+39) 06 4674 2244 from outside.

PICKING UP BASIC SUPPLIES:

Most of our properties are privately owned, so the provisions in the house will vary according to owner. For example, some owners will provide a good supply of toilet paper, soap, and basic food items; others will provide the bare minimum. It is best to expect the latter. Therefore, it is very important to stop at a grocery store prior to arriving at your property for enough supplies to see you through the first day or two. This is doubly important if you are arriving on Saturday, since most stores will be closed on Sunday. For a sample grocery list, keep reading...

GROCERY SHOPPING:

Shopping for food in Italy is a wonderful experience. Major food chains include *Coop* (and *Ipercoop*), *Standa*, *Maxi Sidis*, *Conad*, *SMA*, and *Spar*.

Words for various food shops are: *alimentary* (food-stuff), *supermercato* (supermarket), and *macelleria* (butcher shop). Hint: Check Chapter Five for street markets in your area. Here's a brief rundown of shopping details:

- **Carts:** Many supermarkets lock their carts together. To release a cart, insert a coin into the cart lock. To get your money back, simply re-lock the cart.

- **Payment:** Most stores take credit cards, but some of the smaller grocers may only accept cash.

- **Bagging:** You are expected to bag your own food at the checkout line. A small charge is often applied for plastic bags. Remember to save your grocery bags and reuse them as trash bags at your property!

- **Hours:** Grocery stores generally open each day (except Sunday) at about 8:30 AM and close around 1 PM in the afternoon. They will usually open again later in the afternoon and remain open until 7:30 or 8 PM. Except for large supermarkets in cities, most shops are closed on Sunday.

- **Fruits and Vegetables:** Quality is often better in the small produce-only shops (or local markets) than in the larger supermarkets. PLEASE don't handle the fresh produce! Doing so is considered very bad manners! The shopkeeper will be happy to choose your produce for you. Just point to your desired selection, or use your dictionary. In larger supermarkets, disposable plastic gloves are provided for bagging the produce. There will be an automatic scale for weighing the produce; just plop your selection on the scale, push the corresponding produce button, and a price sticker will be issued. Unless otherwise indicated, all items are sold by the kilo. If you don't see a scale, your produce will be weighed at the checkout counter.

- **Fresh Bread:** Made every night, bread is quickly snatched up in the morning and is often unavailable later in the day. The best place to buy bread is a bakery (*forno* or *panificio*). *Pane Toscano* is unsalted Tuscan bread. A good, soft, salted bread is *Pugliese*.

- **Delicatessen Counters:** Found in most grocery stores, you can easily throw together a picnic or light dinner with items found here: cold cuts, cheese, olives, artichoke hearts, and other *antipasto* items.

- **Decoding dairy products:** You will find milk in aseptic packaging (boxed with no need for refrigeration until opened) in every grocery store. It's quite good. *Latte intero* is whole milk, *latte parzialmente scremato* is low-fat milk, and *latte scremato* is non-fat milk. The yogurt is fabulous. The word for non-fat is *magro*; Danone, Parmalat-Linea Piú, and Vitasnella are all good brands that make tasty non-fat varieties. If you're not looking for non-fat, then Yomo is the best!

SAMPLE SHOPPING LIST:

Do as the Italians do--shop for fresh food and groceries each day! Here's what you'll find in our cart:

☐ water (*acqua con gas* or *naturale*)	☐ bread (*pane*)
☐ milk (*latte*)	☐ pasta (fresh, tortellini)
☐ wine (*vino*)	☐ bottled sauces
☐ olive oil (*olio di uliva*)	☐ salt, pepper, spices
☐ vinegar (*aceto*)	☐ bullion cubes (Knorr)
☐ tea & coffee	☐ yogurt & cold cereal
☐ eggs (*uova*) & chicken (*pollo*)	☐ jam (*marmellata*) & butter (*burro*)
☐ canned beans (*fagioli*), tomatoes (*pomodori*), & tuna (*tonno*)	☐ mushrooms (*porcini*; dried, canned, fresh) & capers (*capperi*)
☐ fruit (*frutta*), including lemons (*limoni*)	☐ basil (*basilico*) & garlic (*aglio*)
☐ deli items: cheese, olives, artichokes, roasted peppers, meats, mozzarella, etc.	☐ vegetables: potatoes, onions, carrots, green beans, tomatoes, peppers, cucumbers, etc.
☐ dish & bar soap	☐ toilet paper & towels
☐	☐

ITALIAN CUISINE:

- **Breakfast:** Breakfast is the least important meal of the day in Italy. It rarely consists of more than coffee, a croissant, or a roll.

- **Lunch:** The most important meal, lunch is a time for families to gather together for a long, leisurely meal, especially on weekends.

- **Aperitivo:** It is customary to stop at a bar for an *aperitivo* before going out to lunch or dinner. *Aperitivo* usually consists of an alcoholic or non-alcoholic drink with chips, olives, or *salatini*.

- **Dinner:** Lighter than lunch, dinner is typically from 8 to 9 PM

- **Restaurants:** The lunch hour usually begins at 12:30 PM, and patrons arriving late may be turned away after 2:00 PM. Italians go out to restaurants to socialize, so don't be surprised if they spend an hour or two at a restaurant or pizzeria. Since a meal may easily last all evening, don't be late if you want a table! Dinner is served beginning at 7:30 PM, but most Italians don't eat until around 9 PM in the summer. When you get a table in a restaurant, it's yours for as long as you want it, and no one will try to hurry you along. This means you'll have to request the check when you want it: "*Il conto per favore.*"

- **Dining Tips:** Here are a few more pointers for dining out.
  - ♦ Don't feel intimidated by the many courses listed on menus. Usually the *secondi piatti* (main courses of meat or fish) are the most expensive, so if you order just a *primo piatto* (pasta and soup course), a vegetable or an *antipasto* (appetizer), and a *contorno* (side dish), you won't spend much. *Insalata mista* is a mixed salad.
  - ♦ In Italy, it's considered polite to begin eating as soon as you're served rather than waiting until others are served.
  - ♦ *Cappuccino* and *caffe latte* are morning beverages. Ordering one after lunch or dinner will brand you as a tourist! More "socially correct" is to order a *caffe macchiato*: espresso with a dollop of steamed milk. Or, try having a straight shot of espresso!
  - ♦ Bread is placed directly on the table, so don't expect a bread plate. Butter (*burro*) is usually not included. The "dipping sauce" of oil and vinegar is not typical, as it is more of an American invention.

♦ The service charge (*servizio*) is usually included in the bill (*conto*), so you're not obligated to leave a tip. Of course, you're certainly free to leave something extra for good service.

SIMPLE ITALIAN RECIPES:

Following are some simple recipes to get you started. Eating breakfast and dinner at home while dining out for lunch is a nice way to experience a town, both its restaurants and its local produce. Two useful books are Faith Willinger's *Eating in Italy: A Traveler's Guide to the Hidden Gastronomic Pleasures of Northern Italy*, and Fred Plotkin's *Italy for the Gourmet Traveler*. Both books include advice on where and when to shop, various regional food specialties, and other helpful hints. You might want to pack a favorite Italian cookbook, along with an assortment of spices.

- **Salade Nicoise all' Italiana:**
    1. Cook some potatoes, eggs, and green beans until done.
    2. Arranged sliced potatoes, eggs, green beans, tuna, canned white beans, tomatoes, roasted red peppers, cucumbers, capers, olives, basil, etc. on a platter.
    3. Drizzle balsamic dressing and olive oil over everything.
    4. Serve with Tuscan bread.
- **Pasta ai Porcini:**
    1. Sauté fresh mushrooms (*porcini*) in oil with garlic. For dried mushrooms, rinse carefully and soak in hot water before sautéing.
    2. Season the mushrooms with salk, pepper, and rosemary.
    3. Serve over pasta with Parmigiano cheese and Tuscan bread, along with one of the following side dishes.
- **Carote all'Agro:** This is a nice side dish.
    1. Grate raw carrots and drizzle with olive oil and lemon juice.
    2. Salt to taste and chill before serving.
- **Vegetable Salad:** Another side dish.
    1. Marinate zucchini, carrot, cucumber, and fennel bulb slices with tomatoes.

- **Penne alla Susanna (a Rentvillas special):**
  1. Toss together cooked penne pasta, canned sun-dried tomatoes (including most of the oil), olives, canned tuna (drained), artichoke hearts, and sliced roasted eggplant. (All can be found in the grocery store.)
  2. Season with salt and balsamic dressing or lemon juice.

- **Minestrone:**
  1. Sauté onions and garlic in olive oil.
  2. Add broth, bring to a boil, and then add a selection of vegetables (carrots, zucchini, peppers, potatoes, celery, etc.) along with canned white beans.
  3. Just before the vegetables are cooked, add pasta and fresh (or frozen) spinach.
  4. Season with your herbs of choice, salt, and pepper.
  5. Serve with Parmigiano cheese, green salad, and Tuscan bread.

- **Insalata alla Californiana:**
  1. Mix canned white beans (drained) with flaked canned tuna, tomatoes, roasted peppers, onions, cucumbers, etc.
  2. Toss with a balsamic dressing, olive oil, crushed garlic, lemon juice, salt, and pepper.

- **Zuppa di Funghi (mushroom soup):**
  1. Sauté onions and garlic in olive oil.
  2. Add 1/2 cup of white or red wine and bring to a boil.
  3. Add coarsely chopped mushrooms.
  4. Add broth (any kind) and bring to a boil.
  5. Lower the heat and add 2 cups of bread, sliced into cubes.
  6. Simmer for 20 minutes, stirring often.
  7. Season with your herbs of choice, as well as salt and pepper. Serve with *Pomodori e Mozzarella*, below.

- **Pomodori e Mozzarella:**
  1. Toss coarsely chopped tomatoes with fresh cubed mozzarella.
  2. Add basil, olive oil, balsamic vinegar, salt, and pepper.
  3. Chill before serving. Can be served over fresh pasta.

- **Zuppa Casalinga:**
    1. Sauté onion, garlic, and lean ground meat in olive oil.
    2. Add one can of large white beans, one can of another variety of bean, canned tomatoes, and a can of tomato sauce. Thin with broth.
    3. Simmer for about 20 minutes, seasoning with oregano, salt, and pepper.
    4. Serve with mixed salad and Tuscan bread.

Pasta con Uova:
1. Saute bread crumbs in oil until crisp.
2. Saute onions and garlic.
3. Cook pasta, drain, and add to onion mixture.
4. Add beaten eggs to pasta and cook gently until almost done.
5. Stir in slivered prosciutto and cook until eggs are set.
6. Top with bread crumbs, capers, cheese, onions, etc. and serve with a mixed salad.

CHAPTER FOUR:
MAKING THE MOST OF YOUR STAY

Now that you've arrived at your property, here are some tips to help you make the most of your stay. If you know what to expect, your travels abroad will be an enriching cultural experience... so go in with an open mind and be ready to learn something new! Review this section to learn about...

…Meeting the key holder/manager

…Etiquette and attitude

…Greetings

…Mosquitoes, screens, and deterrents

…Heating or cooling the house

…Plumbing and electricity

This chapter concludes with a section on **Italian life**. Make sure to browse these topics for helpful hints about daily life in Italy, including banks and money, national holidays, museums and churches, mail and stamps, strikes, your safety, emergency numbers, public bathrooms, beds, laundry, and coffee makers.

MEETING THE KEY HOLDER/MANAGER:

You have now arrived at your property to meet the key holder or manager. Here are some important issues to keep in mind.

- **Language:** What will you do if he/she speaks no English (pretty likely)? Have a pocket dictionary in hand, a sense of humor, and patience! Remember, he/she is used to meeting "foreigners."

- **Contact Info:** Get his/her telephone number for any questions during your stay.

    Name: _____

    Tel.#: _____

- **Appliances:** Get an explanation of the appliances before the keyholder leaves; don't just nod your head and assume that you will figure it out! FYI the washing machines in Europe are generally smaller in size than those in the U.S., and they are more energy efficient (translation: they take up to 2 hours per load). You will sometimes find a clothes dryer, but if so, it will also be small in size and energy efficient.

- **Important Info:** Ask if there is a house book. Otherwise, find out where the nearest market, pharmacy, restaurants, and fun activites are!

- **Trash and Recyling:** Don't expect a garbage-man to arrive at your property! Italy is self-service. Garbage is placed in the big trash containers (*bidone*) that you will see frequently along the roads and city streets. Plastic grocery bags make handy trash bags, so don't throw them away! Recycling is practiced throughout Italy; you will see round-topped green containers for glass (*vetro*) and yellow ones for clean paper and cardboard (*carta*).

- **Fuse box:** Finally, ask for the location of the fuse box and find out what you need to do if the power goes out!

NOTES: _____
_____
_____
_____

ETIQUETTE AND ATTITUDE:

The right frame of mind is very important when living in Italy. You'll encounter plenty of differences, not the least of which are water and/or drain problems, different business hours, strikes, insects, etc. Hopefully, you have a sense of adventure-- after all, one of the reasons you decided to travel to Italy was to experience these cultural differences.

Your sojourn will be most rewarding if you're able to go with the flow! If you're only happy with American standards, you're better off visiting Italy from the relative protection of air-conditioned buses and deluxe or first-class hotels. Renting is for people who really want to know Italy, the Italian people, and understand the concept of *La Dolce Vita!*

GREETINGS:

Italians, and particularly southern Italians, tend to be more formal than Americans with regard to titles. For instance, if an Italian is an engineer, you would address him as *Ingegnere*. If in doubt, it's safe to use the title *Dottore* or *Dottoressa*, since it refers to a graduate of the university, as well as to a medical doctor. In general, it's a title of respect. First names are not used until you have become good friends, or until you have been invited to use them. A formal substitute for *ciao* is *salve*.

MOSQUITOES, SCREENS, and DETERRENTS:

Most Italian homes do not have window screens. The primary reason for this is because they "spoil the view." Beyond that, they simply aren't as important in Italy as they are in America. For this reason, you should come prepared to deal with mosquitoes and other flying insects, particularly in countryside villas.

One helpful device is the *antizanzare elettrico*, a small, inexpensive plug-in device. Small treated tablets, called *piastrine*, are inserted before plugging it into an outlet. Easy to find in most grocery stores, they emit a pleasant smell that will repel insects. Two brands to look for are Baygon and Vape.

Rentvillas recieves dozens of complaints about mosquitoes every year, so please bring repellents with you or plan to purchase some type of protection when you arrive. If you're really allergic, you might also consider bringing some mosquito netting and masking tape to seal off bedroom windows.

HEATING OR COOLING THE HOUSE:

It's important to understand that in Europe, and Italy in particular, energy costs will be much higher than you are accustomed to at home. So if you'll be using either air conditioning or heating, do so conservatively.

During the warmer months, it is common practice to close the shutters in the early part of the day and open them again in the evening. This is an easy and practical way of utilizing the natural construction of the house to keep your environment nice and cool. When you get up in the morning, close up your bedroom on the way out. And if you'll be out exploring for the day, take a few minutes to close up the entire house. You'll be pleasantly surprised when you come home!

If you are traveling during the colder months, try "alternate" methods for keeping warm before you turn up the heat: bring warm socks and/or slippers, make coffee or tea, use the fireplace if one is available, and put any extra blankets on the beds. Also close doors to rooms that aren't in use to prevent heating extra space. Do note that heating is the most expensive utility, so if you are traveling during the winter, adjust your budget to account for the heating bill.

The laws governing the use of central heating are restrictive in the interest of energy conservation. Generally speaking, no heating is allowed from mid-April until the first of November, although this can vary. If your property has a working fireplace, you will probably need to request and pay for firewood. During the spring and fall (and sometimes even in June), it's possible to have quite low temperatures as well as rain... so come prepared!

PLUMBING AND ELECTRICITY:

One of the reasons why we travel to Italy is to enjoy the historic atmosphere created by buildings that have been around for generations. But the price that has to be paid for conserving such structures is a lower standard and a much higher cost for plumbing and electricity.

Builders and remodelers find creative ways to integrate modern technology into these historic buildings, but it's not always perfect-- so if something goes wrong, have a little patience... It's a cultural experience! Call the number on your voucher and your keyholder will do his or her best to resolve the problem.

To avoid having such problems in the first place, think conservatively. Using no more than one or two appliances at a time will save you from blowing a fuse. Try not to take long showers or flush a lot of toilet paper, and make sure the drain is clear of hair after you shower. Water heaters tend to be smaller, so you may not have an endless hot water supply anyway! Lighting will probably also be dimmer than you are used to, so bring a book light. And rather than being central, air conditioning is typically a window unit that will only cool one room.

Energy and water costs are very much higher in Italy, so try to be energy-conscious in whatever you do... particularly if *you* will be paying the costs of your utilities!

ITALIAN LIFE:

Banks: Hours are usually 8:30 AM to 1:30 PM, and then again for one hour in the afternoon (usually 3-4 PM). Many are also open on Saturday from 8:30 AM to 1:30 PM. Otherwise, they are closed on Saturday afternoons, Sundays, and holidays.

Money: In general, the cheapest way to get Euros is with a bank ATM card. Fortunately, there are plenty of ATMs in Italy where you can use your bank card, Visa, MasterCard, or American Express to get money. The ATM will automatically debit your main account. Be aware that the maximum withdrawal amount is usually about 500 Euros, and there will be some sort of transaction cost (higher for credit cards than ATM bank cards). Ask your bank or credit card company for details.

In order to use a card at an ATM machine, your PIN number must have four digits. If you don't have a PIN number for your credit card, call the service number on the back and ask if it is possible to obtain one before your trip.

Many Italian banks have automatic currency exchange machines. These are conveniently located outside banks, in airports, and also in main train stations. They do not accept denominations higher than $50, so bring only $20 and $50 bills. The commission charged for the electronic transaction can be higher than exchanging directly with the bank, in some instances significantly. In any case, it is convenient to carry cash to change as you go. With traveler's checks, you often have to wait in long lines and fill out paperwork to change them for cash. To protect your cash, consider carrying a hidden money belt, easily obtained at most travel supply shops.

Be sure to keep your bank receipts when you change money. You may need these to change your extra Euros back into dollars on your way home.

Museum Hours: Many major museums are now open from 9 AM - 7 PM or later, usually closing on Mondays. Smaller museums will keep their own individual hours. The most popular museums include: in Florence, the Uffizi, the Accademia, and the Pitti Palace; in Rome, the Galleria Borghese, the Palazzo

Altemps, Castel Sant'Angelo, and the Galleria Nazionale Romano; in Venice, the Accademia. To eliminate time spent waiting in long lines, order tickets in advance at **www.tickitaly.com**.

National Holidays: You should expect almost all museums, monuments, shops, and most restaurants to be closed on major national holidays. These include:
- Jan 1,
- May 1 (Labor Day)
- Dec 25

Other holidays, during which many services will be closed, are:
- Jan 6 (Epiphany)
- Easter Monday
- April 25 (Liberation Day)
- June 2 (Anniversary of the Founding of the Republic)
- Aug 15 (Assumption)
- Nov 1 (All Saints)
- Dec 8 (Immaculate Conception)
- Dec 26 (St Stephen's Day).

In addition to these holidays, each town will celebrate the feast-day of its patron saint.

Churches: Strict dress codes apply and entry may be refused if you are wearing shorts or your upper arms are bare. Most churches are dark, so make sure you carry coin pieces for the automatic lights.

Mail/Stamps: Mail delivery in Italy has traditionally been unreliable and erratic. However, it is becoming more efficient. Private companies deliver packages as well as mail, and big cities now have UPS and FedEx. When sending to the U.S., *Posta Prioritaria* (priority mail) works very well. Postage may be purchased in *tabacchi* shops or directly at the post office. Post offices are generally open from 8:30 AM to 2 PM. On Saturdays and the last day of the month, they close at 12 PM. Major post offices in large cities and in airports are open 24 hours a day for registered mail.

Strikes: It's best to adjust your mental attitude on the subject of strikes (*sciopero*) before arriving in Italy: they occur frequently. Strikes are usually announced at least a week ahead of time. During a recent trip, we encountered a train strike, a gas delivery strike, and an airport strike. If you have a definite schedule to follow, be sure to have a "Plan B," or be ready to get creative!

Your Safety: When walking the streets of any city it's smart to guard your pockets, purse, and camera. Italy is no exception. Pay close attention in crowded places such as public transportation centers and outdoor markets... or "quiet hands" might remove your camera or wallet! Don't wear valuables or carry items that might make you a target. If you have a rental car, never leave items visible that might identify you as a tourist, such as maps, guidebooks, cameras, suitcases, etc. Lock personal items in the trunk; consider it cheap insurance to purchase an Italian newspaper and leave it visible in your car. While sightseeing, use a fanny pack or shoulder purse (worn across the body), taking only enough cash and/or a credit card for the day. Using an under-garment passport/cash holder for the rest is always a good idea.

Emergency Numbers:
- 113 - Italian "911"
- 112 - Police (*Carabinieri*)
- 115 - Fire department
- 116 - ACI (Italian Auto Club) Road Assistance
- 118 - Medical emergencies
- 12 - Directory Assistance
- 170 - English speaking operator (wait through the bilingual messages and then dial 2)
- English Yellow Pages are available at English language bookstores in most major cities.

Public bathrooms: Not so widely found in Italy as they are in the States, it takes a little patience to locate them, so look out for restaurants, large cafés and bars, museums, gas stations, and train stations. *Signori* is men; *signore* is women. Restrooms range in quality from standard "American" toilets to porcelain holes in the floor... so be prepared! Keep emergency toilet paper (or a pack of tissues) on hand for when paper is nowhere to be found. In airports, train stations, and *autostrade* restaurants, you may have to pay for entrance with coins.

If you're traveling with children, carry a little packet of hand-wipes to wash up afterwards.

Beds: When it comes to comfort, there's really "no place like home," so don't expect your bed in Italy to be as comfortable (or firm) as your own-- although we're often pleasantly surprised. There are no king- or queen-sized beds in Italian homes; instead, you'll find a *matrimoniale*, which is the same width as a queen (160 cm) but slightly shorter in length. Frequently, you will find that this bed is composed of two 80 cm single beds shoved together and sheeted as one. Single beds are the same or slightly narrower than the US standard. In a few cases, you will find what Italians call a "French bed," which is similar to a standard double bed, usually about 140 cm wide. Europeans seem to feel that the "French bed" is adequate for two people, but many Americans disagree!

Laundry: Look for the sign *"tintoria"* for cleaning and pressing, *"lavanderia"* for laundry, or *"lavasecco"* for drycleaning. Washing machines are smaller and more energy efficient than those in the US. Cycles can take up to 2 hours, so don't be in a hurry. In addition, be aware that the temperatures listed on the panel are in Celsius; you'd be wise to stay below 40 degrees. For safety reasons, the door will remain locked for a couple of minutes once the cycle is over, so be patient. Don't force it open! As for dryers, they are rare in Italy. Everyone hangs laundry on wire racks or lines.

Coffee Makers: Italians make their coffee in small quantities, using an espresso grind and a "Moka." The Moka looks like a skinny metal teapot and consists of two sections screwed together. These coffee makers come in a variety of sizes, and at least one can be found in every kitchen. To make coffee, fill the removable basket (this is the filter) with finely ground coffee. Then fill the bottom section with water and replace the basket; the water level should come up to just below the basket. Screw the two sections together tightly so they won't leak under pressure. Place the Moka directly on the burner and heat on high until the water boils. Just after it starts to boil, remove from the fire. Stir, then pour your freshly brewed espresso! The most popular coffee brands are Lavazza, Caffe Kimbo, and Illy Caffe.

IN THE FOLLOWING PAGES:

Cities of Italy
- Rome 55
- Florence 61
- Venice 67

Regions of Italy
- Tuscany 73
- Umbria 83
- Cinque Terre (& Italian Riviera) 87
- Italian Lakes 91
- Veneto 97
- Amalfi Coast 101
- Sicily 109

CHAPTER FIVE:
CITIES OF ITALY

Whether you're renting an urban apartment or staying in a countryside villa, odds are that you'll end up spending at least some of your time exploring one of Italy's three most popular cities: Rome, Florence, and Venice.

In the following pages you'll find a broad range of information on each city, from recommended restaurants and museums to local markets and navigational tips. Each city has been divided into three sections: orientation, culture, and sights.

Remember as you plan your excursion that all three of these cities are best seen on foot or via public transportation, so wear comfortable walking shoes. And don't just hurry from one sight to another... take time to enjoy the atmosphere right where you are. Tuck the map in your pocket. Wander!

ROME

Rome is not for the faint-of-heart: it's a boisterous city of 2,900,000 that overflows with more history, art, and culture than arguably any other city in the world. Coexisting seamlessly with the beat of modern Roman life are relics from classical, early Christian, Baroque, Romanesque, Renaissance, Rococo, and post-Unification eras. Each of the city's neighborhoods, from Trastevere to E.U.R., has its own distinct flavor and rhythm. Wherever you are in the city, Rome has a dizzying array of sights, including such historic heavyweights as the Colosseum, the Pantheon, and the Roman Forum-- enough to occupy even the most zealous traveler for months.

ORIENTATION:

Hotel: If you're just passing through, we can recommend two clean, reasonably-priced hotels near the Campo dei Fiore. One is the Albergo del Sole (Via del Biscione 76, 00186 Roma; Tel. (+39) 06 6880 6873). Website: www.solealbiscione.it The other is the Hotel Pomezia (Via dei Chiavari 13, 00186 Roma; Tel. (+39) 06 6861 371). Website: www.hotelpomezia.it

Bus/Metro Tickets: You can buy a pack of bus tickets, which also function as metro tickets, at Termini Train Station or in any *tabacchi* in the city. The *Biglietto Integrato a Tempo* (B.I.T.) lasts for 75 minutes from the time it is validated. Unfortunately the bus system in Rome is very complicated, with over 200 routes and no English website. If you speak Italian, try www.atac.roma.it; otherwise, be prepared to wing it! Ask locals, other travelers, and bus drivers... eventually, you'll find your way! If you find yourself needing to meet a deadline, however, take a cab.

English Bookstore: Visit the Anglo-American Bookshop at Via dell Vite 102 (near the Spanish Steps). Tel. (+39) 06 678 4347. Website: www.aab.it

CULTURE:

Local Events: For local news, concerts, events, classifieds, and lots of other info, check out www.wantedinrome.com

Museum Pass: The Roma Pass is a 3-day pass that covers transportation, free admission into your first two museums, and offers discounts on others. It can be obtained at most tourist information booths, museums, and at the airport. Website: www.romapass.it

Market: The Piazza Campo dei Fiori has a wonderful open-air market where you can buy fresh fruits, vegetables, fish, and flowers in the morning (except Sunday). In the evening you can enjoy outdoor dining and various forms of entertainment from street performers. There are also several great gelato places in the area!

Restaurant Recommendation: Of course there are many wonderful restaurants in Rome, but the Trattoria Othello alla Concordia is a special find from a Rome native. It offers authentic Italian food, but may be very crowded in the summer due to its location near the Spanish Steps! (Via della Croce 81; Tel. (+39) 06 679 1178)

Walking Tours: Context Travel offers a really unique way to see Florence, Rome, or Naples. Walk through the city with an architect, historian, or art expert to see these cities in a whole new way. www.contexttravel.com

SIGHTS:

Saint Peter's Basilica: The most prominent building within the Vatican city, this enormous church is fantastic as an architectural marvel. It also features famous works of art such as Michelangelo's *Pieta*, Bernini's *Baldacchino,* and St. Peter's chair. Admission is free, but you must dress appropriately (knees and shoulders covered). It is usually open from 7 AM to 6 PM (7 PM April through September). The cupola of the gigantic dome (designed by Michelangelo) offers 360-degree views of the city; an elevator goes to the base of the dome, but you'll have to walk the rest of the way! This is slightly claustrophobic, and you should bring water.

The Colosseum: The famous arena where gladiators battled to the death, the Colosseum is majestic even in ruins. Keep in mind that you'll have to wait in line, although it usually moves quickly. It's open every day at 9 AM, except for Christmas and New Year's, and closes anywhere from 4:30 PM to 7:30 PM depending on the time of year (hours are shorter in the winter).

Villa Borghese: Pronounced "bor-gay-zee," this beautiful park sits in the center of Rome (near the Piazza Navona) and is crisscrossed with trails for walking, jogging, bicycling, and skating. The Galleria Borghese houses one of the world's most extensive art collections, featuring paintings and sculptures by Raphael, Rubens, Titian, Caravaggio, Bernini, and Canova. Because museum capacity is limited, reservations are necessary for admission. To make a reservation call: (+39) 06 32810 or (for a slightly higher price) purchase tickets online at www.tickitaly.com. Just remember to pick up and pay for your reserved tickets at least half an hour before your admission time. You can also stop by the museum earlier in the week to purchase tickets for a later date. The museum is open Tuesday-Sunday from 9 AM to 7 PM.

Fontana di Trevi: The Trevi Fountain is one of the most beautiful fountains in Rome. Famous not only for its artistic significance, the fountain was the site of Anita Ekberg's dip in Fellini's 1960 film, *La Dolce Vita*. The small square can often be ridiculously crowded, but a glimpse of the fountain is well worth the hassle, and particularly beautiful at night. Don't forget to throw a coin over your shoulder and wish for a return trip to Rome! Hint: Skip the gelato in this area! A single scoop costs an arm and a leg.

Piazza Navona: This square is home to three beautiful fountains, including Bernini's Fountain of the Four Rivers (*Fontana dei Quattro Fiumi*). Many street artists like to set up shop and paint portraits here as well. This is an ideal spot for an *espresso* or an *aperitivo*. Sit, drink, and take in the scene.

Roman Forum: The site of many ancient Roman ruins and temples, the Foro Romano is an amazing place to explore, perfect for just after you've seen the nearby Colosseum. The place is always full of tour guides doing their thing... you'd be surprised at the fascinating historical tidbits you can pick up just by strolling within earshot of the experts!

The Pantheon: This ancient temple has a perfectly spherical dome; built more than a millennium ago, it is still in excellent condition.

The Piazza di Spagna: The Spanish Steps are a fun place to sit, relax, and people-watch. In the summer months, you'll find the steps packed with a young, hip, international crowd-- and you may even be witness to a wedding or two! If you're in Rome to shop, the surrounding area features the best in Italian *alta moda*.

Mouth of Truth: Famous for its part in the classic film *Roman Holiday* (starring Gregory Peck and Audrey Hepburn), legend says that the Bocca della Verita will bite your hand off if you stick it in and tell a lie! Note that the mouth is located inside the portico of the church of Santa Maria in Cosmedin, so you won't see it from the street.

Tarot Garden: Created by the artist Niki de Sainte Phalle, *Il Giardino dei Tarrochi* features monumental sculptures. Located outside of Rome near Garavicchio, it makes an excellent day trip. Website: **www.nikisaintphalle.com**

FLORENCE

A city of many layers, Florence is at once an overrun tourist magnet and a living, breathing medieval city that is home to proud Florentines. Stomping ground of Michelangelo, Leonardo da Vinci, Dante, and Machiavelli, its cultural importance can't be overstated. It is home to three of the world's most renowned museums: the Uffizi, L'Accademia, and the Bargello, and boasts an incredible number of important churches, which house equally important master works. Sights such as the Ponte Vecchio, the Boboli Gardens, the Pitti Palace, and Brunelleschi's Duomo are but a few of Florence's many offerings. A walker's city, the center of Florence is a compact labyrinth of alleys and piazze. Comfortable shoes are a must! Delve into the historic center to explore myriad shops, museums and charming restaurants.

ORIENTATION:

Street Addresses: Each street has two sets of numbers: Red numbers indicate a shop, restaurant, or business; blue numbers indicate a private residence or hotel. Each set has its own sequence, so a red #10 could be next to a blue #23. This also explains why some buildings, with shops on the ground floor and residences above, have two numbers.

Local Info: For comprehensive information on shows, art, movies, events, culture, and everything else Florence has to offer, visit the exuberant www.vivifirenze.it, which caters to a younger crowd, or the more stately www.comune.fi.it/inglese.

English Bookstore: Check out McRae books, located on Via de' Neri 32R. Website: www.mcraebooks.com

International Products: Pegna grocery shop offers a wide variety of international foods, wines, hygiene products, etc. (Via dello Studio 8; Tel. (+39) 5528 2701)

Plane/Train Reservations: If you need either one in a hurry, go to the American Express office on Via Dante. They speak English and are very helpful.

Parking: The best policy is simply to avoid cars in Florence (use public transport if you venture out of town), but if you have no choice, you'll need to deal with parking. Don't even try to park on the street; most parking is by permit only. Beyond that, the streets are cleaned each week. If your car is in the way, it will be towed and you'll have to pay to get it back! Here are four convenient, supervised garages: Piazza Stazione (this handy underground parking is located in front of the train station), Porta Romana (Oltrarno), Fortezza da Basso, and Piazza Liberta (underground parking).

CULTURE:

Museum Reservations: To avoid long lines, remember to make reservations for visiting museums. Visit **www.tickitaly.it** or **www.florenceart.it**.

Shop: There are literally thousands of wonderful shops of all types throughout Florence, but there is one not to miss. The Officina Profumo Farmaceutica di Santa Maria Novella (Via della Scala) is located within a beautiful historic building. It sells perfumes, soaps, colognes, and other fragrant products that have been made according to the same recipes for centuries. It's the perfect place to buy a unique gift.

Central Market: In the historical center near the San Lorenzo church, this huge building is host to countless market stalls featuring fresh meats, vegetables, fruits, and other goodies you might need for making your own delectable Italian meals. Open Monday - Friday 7 AM until 2 PM, and Saturday 4 PM to 8 PM. It's certainly worth a visit (or three) if you plan to do any cooking during your stay. Take a backpack or a sturdy bag to stow your produce.

Other Markets: In Piazza Ghiberti (Santa Croce district), you'll find a great farmer's market open Monday through Saturday from 7 AM to 2 PM. On the third Sunday of each month, the Fierucola (Organic Market) is held in the Piazza Santo Spirito. You can buy organic wines, olive oil, cheese, bread, etc.

Theatre: The Maggio Musicale Fiorentino runs throughout may and June in Florence, offering operas, ballets, and concerts. Visit www.maggiofiorentino.com for information, schedules, and tickets. The concert season opens in mid-October at the Teatro Communale, while opera kicks off in mid-December.

Mass in English: The Duomo has a mass in English Saturdays at 5:30 PM.

Movies in English: The Odeon Cinema in Piazza Strozzi offers English films every Monday and Tuesday.

Walking Tours: Context Travel offers a really unique way to see Florence, Rome, or Naples. Walk through the city with an architect, historian, or art expert to see these cities in a whole new way. www.contexttravel.com

Cooking Class: La Cucina del Garga offers a fun one-day cooking class in Florence. www.garga.it

Restaurants: There are so many excellent restaurants in Florence that it's impossible to list them all, but here are a few favorites.
- *Enoteca Pane e Vino* is a trendy, expensive restaurant west of the Arno. Via San Niccolo 60-70/r; Tel. (+39) 055 247 6956.
- *Paoli* has become a bit of a tourist destination in recent years, but it never fails to deliver great food, Old-World ambiance, and no-nonsense service. Via dei Tavolini 12/2; Tel. (+39) 055 216215.
- *Mamma Gina* serves very good food at excellent prices and has an Italian family clientele. It is located on the far side of the Ponte Vecchio. Borgo San Jacopo 37/r; Tel. (+39) 055 239 6009.
- *La Sostanza* serves good Tuscan food in a very casual setting; popular with Florentines and tourists alike. Via del Porcellana 25/r; Tel. (+39) 055 212691.
- *Garga* is a hip restaurant featuring frescoed walls, surrealist décor, wonderful food presentation, and lively service. It's a hopping place, so be sure to make reservations! Via del Moro 48; Tel. (+39) 055 239 8898.

- *Trattoria Belle Donne* is a tiny, crowded trattoria with excellent food. First-come, first-served, so arrive early. Via delle Belle Donne 16/r; Tel. (+39) 055 238 2609.
- *Boccadama* is a nice wine bar that offers snacks and light dinners. Piazza Santa Croce 25-26r; Tel. (+39) 055 243640.

SIGHTS:

The Museum of the History of Science: A fascinating place for all ages, the Museo di Storia della Scienza is located very close to the Uffizi, right along the Arno. The museum includes many of the original experimental devices used by Galileo... along with his finger! Website: **www.imss.fi.it**

Brancacci Chapel: Within the Church of the Carmine, these newly restored frescoes by Masacchio are really worth a visit. Piazza del Carmine.

Bargello Museum: A huge collection of important Renaissance sculptures. Via del Proconsolo 4.

Museo San Marco: A former Dominican convent, this museum features cells painted by Fra Angelico in addition to being a perfectly preserved example of convent architecture. Piazza San Marco.

Museo Davanzati: Decorated and furnished as a medieval family house. Via Porta Rossa.

Museo del' Opera del Duomo: Located directly behind the Duomo, this is truly a gem of a museum. It houses the works that were originally displayed outside the baptistery and the cathedral. Not to be missed!

Church of Santa Maria Novella: A beautiful church located near the train station, with newly restored frescos by Ghirlandaio and others.

Vasarian Corridor: If you can manage to get in, this is a special treat. The Corridoio Vasariano is an old passage that connects the Uffizi to the Palazzo Pitti via a corridor that extends across the river through the Ponte

Vecchio at the second story level. It houses room after room of important paintings that are seldom seen by the public. Visit **www.florenceart.it** to make a reservation. Click on the "Galleria degli Uffizi," and then on "Vasarian Corridor with Guide." There will be certain dates listed when the tour is available.

VENICE

Inspired by the Greek and Arab cities of the early Middle Ages, Venice is built across 118 islands. It is a bewitching maze of alleys, bridges, canals, and piazze. Long a cultural center, the Venetian school bred high renaissance masters such as Titian and Tintoretto; the city's art collection is rivaled only by that of Florence. Piazza San Marco is perhaps one of the finest medieval squares in Europe. The dialect of Venice is without comparison and is virtually undecipherable to the uninitiated: for example, *rio'* means "canal," while *rio' terra* means "filled-in canal." Spring's renowned *Carnevale* is celebrated in distinctive masquerade and commemorated with theatrical spectacles. The Biennale, the world's most famous contemporary art show, draws an urbane, international crowd to Venice every other year.

ORIENTATION:

Arrival: If you drive to Venice, you must leave your car in one of the huge parking areas at the Piazzale Roma prior to taking a *vaporetto* (waterbus) into the center. Should you plan to return your rental car prior to taking a boat into the city, make sure you know ahead of time where the car rental agency is located. Some of the agencies are in the Piazzale Roma; others, however, are located at the train station in the town of Mestre, a few miles before you reach Venice. Possibly the best way to arrive in Venice is by train, because the train station faces onto the Grand Canal and from there you can either walk or take a vaporetto to your destination in the city.

Navigating: Venice is a maze of winding streets which seem to have no rhyme or reason. Instead of spending an hour studying your map, tuck it into your pocket and wander for five hours. Let your feet take you where they will-- then take out your map and try to get back "home." This is an excellent way to begin to understand this amazing city. Another suggestion is to explore only one *sestiere* (section or neighborhood) a day. There are six Venetian *sestieri:* San Marco, Castello, Dorsoduro, San Polo, Santa Croce, and Cannaregio. There is enough to see and do in each *sestieri* to keep you occupied for the entire day and then some! Most visitors to Venice hit the Piazza San Marco and the Rialto Bridge and figure that they've seen the sights. Not so!

Avoid the Crowds: Investigate the neighborhoods outside of the main tourist areas. You'll discover the authentic Venice: a place where children play in small squares and laundry flutters on lines stretched across narrow canals. It is a quiet and peaceful Venice, where people live and tourists rarely venture. Of course, it's impossible to avoid the crowds altogether. If, however, you plan your trips carefully to the major tourist sites, you can decrease your chances of being overrun by the masses. Scheduling museum trips about an hour or so before lunch time is quite effective. At that time, most of the tour groups are on their way out of the museums and on to the restaurants. You should have a good hour to explore before the museum closes.

CULTURE:

Concerts, Opera, and Dance: Posters advertising concerts, ballets, and various other forms of entertainment are plastered everywhere in Venice. Purchase a ticket and go enjoy a show! Listening to Bach or Vivaldi in a beautiful church, such as the 14th century Santo Stefano, is an experience bordering on the truly divine!

Carnival: If you're visiting during *Carnivale*, you're in for the experience of a lifetime! Get all of your news and updates from the official site at **www.carnevale.venezia.it**.

Restaurants: Here are a couple of suggestions to get you started!
- *Vino Vino* is a wine bar located near the La Fenice Theatre. It is a fun, inexpensive little spot to have a simple lunch and drink good wine. San Marco 2007/A; Tel. (+39) 041 2417688. Website: **www.vinovino.co.it**
- *Da Fiore* offers an upscale lunch or dinner in an elegant setting. It has delicious seafood and is frequented by natives. Calle del Scaleter 2202 (near Campo S. Polo).

SIGHTS:

Highlights of the Six Sestieri: Any guidebook (Eyewitness and Cadogan are both good) will give you a full description of the main sights in each of the six districts of Venice. Here are a few sure bets!
- *San Marco:* The Doge's Palace, the Basilica of San Marco, the Campanile, the Correr Museum, La Fenice Theater.
- *Castello:* The Arsenale, Naval History Museum, San Giorgio Schiavoni (Carpaccio paintings), the Church of San Giovanni e Paolo, the Byzantine Art Museum.
- *Dorsoduro:* The Academia, Ca' Rezzonico, Santa Maria della Salute, the Peggy Guggenheim Museum.
- *San Polo & Santa Croce:* Ca' Pesaro (Museum of Modern Art), the Rialto Bridge and market area, the Frari (work by Titian), School of San Rocco.
- *Cannaregio:* The Ca' d Oro, Jewish Ghetto.

The Islands: Plan to spend at least one day (two is better) visiting the outer islands, including Burano, Torcello, Murano, the Lido, etc. The boat trip (probably on a two-tiered *motonave*) to the various islands is relaxing, fun, and helps you gain a better perspective on Venice.

Il Burchiello: This company offers boat trips on the Brenta river, running from Venice to Padua. You'll visit several of the Palladian villas along the way. The outing is expensive, but well worth the money. The trip can be booked through the American Express office near the Piazza San Marco or online at **www.ilburchiello.it**.

70 • Regions of Italy

CHAPTER SIX:
REGIONS OF ITALY

From the alpine beauty of the northern lakes to the spice of Sicily in the south, Italy has many distinct regions, each known for its own individual customs, products, and foods.

In the following pages, you'll find tips and suggestions for enhancing your experience wherever you are. Each region has been divided into **activities** you may want to particpate in, **places** to visit, and any important **details**. Browse the section for the region where you'll be staying, and any adjacent regions as well... you might find some excellent day-trip choices!

IN THIS SECTION:

Tuscany	73
Umbria	83
Cinque Terre (& Italian Riviera)	87
Italian Lakes	91
Veneto	97
Amalfi Coast	101
Sicily	109

TUSCANY

A hilly region rich in agriculture, Tuscany was the home of the Etruscan civilization, and later the birthplace of the Renaissance. It's known for charming, historic towns like Siena, Arezzo, Cortona, Lucca, San Gimignano, and Volterra. A destination for gourmands and enophiles, the wines of Tuscany's Chianti region are famous around the globe. Extra virgin Tuscan olive oil, a staple in regional cuisine, is also highly prized. Tuscany's capital, Florence, is a great art center whose *centro storico* remains closely linked to its past in spite of tourist crowds. The region's Tyrrhenian coast is famous for its white sand beaches and pine forests. All of this just begins to explain why Tuscany has sustained such enduring popularity over the years, and continues to be a highlight of any visit to Italy.

ACTIVITIES:

Private Tours: These tour companies provide everything from sightseeing and outlet shopping to wineries and authentic meals. Check out each company to see what specialties they offer.

- *Maurizio* provides driving and walking tours throughout Tuscany. A native Florentine, his passion for Tuscan history and lore is absolutely infectious. Website: www.MaurizioBellini.com
- *Vitaly* offers the best of Tuscany's food and drink! Website: www.vitaly.it
- *Accidental Tourist* offers real-life experiences in Tuscany that give you the opportunity to enjoy being part of the community rather than "just a tourist." Cooking classes and more. Website: www.AccidentalTourist.com
- *La Dolce Vita* provides sightseeing by car with your own English-speaking driver and guide. City walking tours are also available. Website: www.LaDolceVitaTours.com
- *One Step Closer* has it all: tours of private art collections, medieval villas, museums, art courses, art restoration lessons, cooking classes, wine tasting, and personalized jaunts. Website: www.OneStepCloser.net

Florence Cooking Class: Great for a day-trip, La Cucina del Garga offers a fun one-day cooking class in Florence. **www.garga.it**

Hot Air Balloon: Surely one of the most exhilarating ways to view the landscape! Try **www.FlyBaloon.it** or **www.balloonintuscany.com**.

Biking Tours: One of the best ways to fully enjoy the beauty of the Tuscan countryside is from the seat of a bicycle. If you're not familiar with the lay of the land, having a guide will enhance your experience as well. Here are a couple of recommended companies:
- *I Bike Italy*, headed by Bill Dillon, has put together several single-day bike rides (and walking tours) from Florence. Prices, which are reasonable, include pick-up and drop-off shuttles in the city center, bikes, helmets, water bottles, food, winery visits, and of course a guide. Website: **www.ibikeitaly.com**
- *Best Tuscan Tours* specializes in private and group bike tours throughout Tuscany. Website: **www.BestTuscanTours.it**

Wines: As you may be aware, some of the world's best wines are produced in Tuscany! Many visitors book an organized wine-tasting tour, but it's not necessary. Should you be driving around the countryside, you will certainly spot signs for *cantina venditta diretta* and *azienda vinicola*. Feel free to stop in-- some have tasting rooms where, for a few Euros, you can sample the estate's products. Don't feel like you have to be an expert to enjoy wine tasting, either! Here are a few points to keep in mind: The *Chianti Classico*, from the region between Florence and Siena, is often enjoyed while still young, while the *Chianti Classico Riserva* must be aged in oak for two years before bottling. *Chianti Rufina* is from the area north of the Arno, near Rufina, Petrognano, and Bossi. The full-bodied *Vino Nobili di Montepulciano* and *Brunello di Montalcino* both come from southern Tuscany, below Siena. The only notable white wine is *Vernaccia*, from the area around San Gimignano. The dessert wine, *Vin Santo*, is also produced in Tuscany. It is made from semi-dried grapes. A very popular dessert is to dunk *cantuccini* or *biscotti* into a small glass of *Vin Santo*. For a more detailed primer on Tuscan wines, visit **www.winecountry.it/regions/tuscany**.

Opera: What better place to enjoy opera than Italy? For a calendar of seasonal operas throughout Tuscany, visit **www.toscanaoperafestival.com**.

Sculpture Park: North of Siena, this is great for an afternoon's exercise. Artists from five continents have created sculptures placed throughout this large woodland park. Website: **www.chiantisculpturepark.it**

PLACES:

Tuscany offers endless opportunities for visiting gorgeous historical and natural wonders. The following are some of our favorite destinations beyond the hustle and bustle of Florence. They are arranged in alphabetical order.

Arezzo: A charming town with wonderful art and history, Arezzo is frequently bypassed by tourists. Known for its jewelry and antiques, the center of Arezzo was used in the filming of Roberto Benigni's *Life is Beautiful*. Once one of the most important Etruscan cities, today Arezzo is beautiful for an array of architecture spanning centuries, from Etruscan ruins to the Roman amphitheatre and the Medici Fortress. The first weekend of each month brings a popular antique fair in the Piazza Granda; annually, there is a festival called "Joust of the Saracens," where citizens dress in medieval attire and knights representing each part of the city charge at a target representing a Saracen king. La Buca di San Francesco, located in the frescoed cellar of a 14th-century palazzo, is a great place to eat. Tel. (+39) 0575 23271. Website: **www.bucadisanfrancesco.it**. Market day is Saturday.

Castellina in Chianti: Although it's got a tourist information office and a number of tourist shops, for the most part Castellina is a sleepy little Tuscan village. Along the single main street you'll encounter a church with a lovely skirt of steps, and if you continue along you'll also find a small castle and museum. Life seems to go at a very slow pace here, and there are as many locals as tourists. Stop at Albergaccio di Castellina for a gourmet lunch or dinner (Tel. (+39) 0577 741042; closed Sunday).

To learn all you ever wanted to know about olive oil, sign up for one of Franco Lombardi's seminars. Every Tuesday, Franco conducts a seminar on the finer points of extra-virgin olive oil. He also produces one of the finest extra-virgin, hand-pressed, unfiltered oils in the world (the best, as far as he is concerned)! He is passionate about his product and is a funny, dynamic speaker. The class is taught on his farm, just south of town. To sign up for a seminar, contact: **oliveoil@chiantionline.com** or call (+39) 0577 738 658. Website: **www.oliveoil.chiantionline.com/seminar.htm.** Market day is Saturday morning.

Chianciano Terme: If you're into spas, look no further. People come here from all over the world to be massaged, rubbed, exercised, and to drink the waters. Spa Deus is a high-end spa located up the hill from the main drag. European spas are quite different from American spas, so be prepared for a more casual attitude toward nudity and a more clinical (i.e. less atmospheric) approach to the spa experience. You can call the spa to arrange for a full- or half-day of activities (Tel. (+39) 0578 63232; email **spadeus@comcast.net**). Outside of the modern city is the old town, which is worth a visit; don't miss the Etruscan museum! Market day is Wednesday.

Chiusi: Here you'll find a wonderful archaeological museum as well as some painted Etruscan tombs nearby. It's a pretty drive to Lago di Chiusi, just a few kilometers northeast of town. La Fattoria is a charming ivy-covered hotel and restaurant with good food and views of the lake. If you've ever wanted to try eel (a specialty of the area), this is a good place to do it. Market day is Tuesday.

Cortona: A beautiful hill town close to Arezzo and Lake Trasimeno, Cortona is a "must see." If the name sounds familiar, it's because Frances Mayes' *Under the Tuscan Sun* put Cortona on the map. Built high on a hill, this city is absolutely beautiful from below... and once you get to the top, there are simply marvelous vistas over the entire valley. A couple of main streets feed into a charming piazza, and at the edge of the historic center there is a lovely public garden with fantastic views. Cortona is, however, a town for walkers. Streets run either uphill or down, and there are plenty of historic sights dotting the hillside just begging to be explored on foot. Be prepared to hike up to the Chiesa di Santa Margherita, and then down to the Piazza della Repubblica and the Piazza del Duomo. La Loggetta is a lovely restaurant on the main piazza. The dishes are presented with artistry and the food is very good. Market day is Saturday morning.

Fiesole: Coming from Florence, take bus #7 to Fiesole. It's a short 25-minute trip to this charming town, filled with interesting places to visit (Archeological Zone), invigorating walks (Via S. Francesco to the Monastero di San Francesco, or along the hill behind the Palazzo Pretorio) and fun restaurants. The Pizzeria Etrusca in the town square is excellent! Halfway up the hill to Fiesole (on bus #7, the stop is San Domenico) is the church of San Domenico, near which is a very good pizzeria, Ristorante San Domenico. It's a favorite meeting spot for locals, so you'll need to get there early to secure a table. If you're in Fiesole in July or August, try to get tickets for a performance (concerts, dance and movies) in the Roman Amphitheater. Information on upcoming shows can be found at **www.estatefiesolana.com**.

Greve in Chianti: This medium-sized town is a wine-lover's paradise. The main square, Piazza Matteotti, is lined with shops featuring every accoutrement your favorite vintage could ever need. There are also a number of shops featuring handmade wooden items and small ceramic novelties. You can go into the Chiesa Santa Croce, at the head of the Piazza, or hike up a steep hill to the Franciscan monastery. Visit Le Cantine di Greve-in-Chianti, a large *enoteca* with over 140 wines. (Galleria delle Cantine 2, Tel. (+39) 055 854 6404; open 10AM–8PM) Website: **www.lecantine.it**. Market day is Saturday.

Lucca: An excellent choice for a half-day visit, Lucca is an old walled city whose center is entirely pedestrian. Drive through one of the gates in the wall to the central parking area and then strike out on foot. The Duomo di San Martino and the Church of San Michele in Foro are both gorgeous examples of period architecture, while the Casa di Puccini, where the composer was born, has been transformed into a small museum in his honor. You can also climb the 130 foot Torre Guinigi, but on the other hand viewing the tree-topped tower from below might be just as enjoyable... and a lot less work! Try the restaurant Buca di Sant'Antonio (Via della Cervia 1; Tel. (+39) 058 355881). A short drive from town in Pieve S. Stefano, Vipore is a fine restaurant recommended highly by clients. The Puccini Opera festival takes place each July/August. For more information, visit **www.puccinifestival.it**. Market days are Wednesday and Saturday on the Via dei Bacchettoni.

Montalcino: This is a beautiful hill town to explore, known primarily for its fine Brunello wine. Sights include the Duomo of San Salvatore, the Piazza del Popolo with the Palazzo Communale, and the Church of San Francesco with frescoes by Vincenzo Tamagni. It's also worthwhile to visit the breathtaking 12th century Romanesque church of Sant'Antimo, nearby. You might be fortunate to arrive during a service when the church resonates with Gregorian chants. The interior of the church is made of white travertine and alabaster. (Gregorian chant prayers held Sun-Fri at 9 AM, 12:45, 2:45, 7, and 9 PM) The *Sagre de Tardo* (Festival of the Thrush), a costumed archery contest, is held at the castle on the last Sunday of October. Try the Castello di Banfi winery and its restaurant (Tel. (+39) 0577 840111; reservations are necessary). Market day is Friday from 7AM–1PM on Viale della Liberta.

Montepulciano: Located on a limestone ridge 600 meters above sea level, this town is the source of the famous Vino Nobile wine and other food products such as pork, cheese, and honey. If you don't mind a little exercise, park your car as you enter town and walk up the hill to the Piazza Grande. Sights include the Communal Palace, the Palazzo Tarugi, and the 16th century church of Santa Maria delle Grazie. Try La Grotta, directly across from the beautiful San Biagio church at the foot of the hill (Tel. (+39) 0578 757607). Another good bet is La Chiusa in Montefollonico, a nearby village (88 Via della Madonnina; Tel: (+39) 0577 669668). The Cantiere Internazionale d'Arte is an international workshop and festival of art, music, and theatre (Piazza Grande 7; Tel. (+39) 0578 757089). Website: **www.fondazionecantiere.it**. Market day is Thursday.

Monteriggioni: Just off the superstrada (about 10 km north of Siena), this incredibly picturesque walled town is a great stop for lunch or dinner. It is also particularly nice in the early morning before the tour busses arrive. Located in the piazza, Il Pozzo serves delicious regional dishes (Tel. (+39) 0577 304127; closed Sunday evenings and Monday).

After your meal, stroll around the outside of the wall or climb to the top for a view of the countryside.

Panzano: Located midway between Greve, Castellina, and Radda, this is a charming little town that began as a medieval castle and still retains some of the original towers and walls today. It is notable for a number of local restaurants that are simply divine. Have a tasty meal at the upscale Il Vescovino (Tel. (+39) 055 852464; closed Tuesdays) or at Pietrafitta (Tel. (+39) 0577 741123), on the Panzano road from Castellina. Markets are held every Sunday morning (until 1PM) in the main square.

Pienza: This lovely little town has only recently been rediscovered by tourists (including Italians). The main street is filled with shops selling cheese, sausages, honey, preserves, health foods, spices of all kinds, antiques, ceramics, and leather-work. There are numerous restaurants from which to choose. The history of Pienza (or Citta di Pio) is closely linked to Pope Pius II, known as the great humanist. In 1458 he transformed this ancient town, his birthplace, into a perfect example of architectural and urban design. The area around Pienza includes the castle of Monticchiello. Market day is Friday.

Pisa: Known, of course, for its famous leaning tower (neighbored by the gorgeous 14th century Cathedral of Pisa), the rest of Pisa can be overlooked by undiscerning visitors. Poetry lovers will want to visit Shelley's house and Lord Byron's palace (now the City Archive). There is also a medieval town center, the house of Galileo, countless restaurants, cafes, and... gelato! Market days are Wednesday and Saturday in Via Buonarroti and Via S. Martino.

Radda in Chianti: A characteristic medieval village, Radda is centered about the 14th century church of San Nicolo and the Palazzo Pretorio. Just outside this village, wine lovers will find the Chianti Classico consortium headquarters. Just east of the village, the Ristorante Le Vigne is a good choice for a sample of Tuscan home cooking (Tel. (+39) 0577 738640; closed Mondays). Also nearby is the Badia a Coltibuono, an old abbey that has been transformed into a winery. Drive out for lunch (the restaurant is located in an outbuilding) and then take a walk through the woods. On the way back you can purchase a bottle of the excellent Badia a Coltibuono Chianti wine or olive oil at the shop near the road. Website: **www.coltibuono.com**. Market day is the fourth Monday of each month.

San Gimignano: Known for its soaring towers and narrow pedestrian streets, this walled town is a perfect medieval jewel with museums and churches to explore. However, if you're looking for that "authentic" Italian experience, you won't find it here. Because of its beauty, it has been overrun with tourists; when you arrive, you'll find three huge parking lots dominating the space outside the city walls! The main streets are lined with shops and restaurants, which creates a "Disneylandish" atmosphere. Nevertheless, San Gimignano is unarguably beautiful! In fact, the countryside surrounding the town presents some of the most beautiful views in the region. Those in the know will tell you that the most magical time to visit San Gimignano is in the evening, after all of the tour busses have gone home. Aside from the Collegiata, don't miss the frescos by Gozzoli in the Chiesa di Sant' Agostino. Dorandó is an elegant (if pricey) restaurant with innovative dishes (Tel. (+39) 0577 941862). Market day is Thursday, 8AM–1PM in the Piazze delle Erbe.

San Quirico d'Orcia: This pretty little town is empty of tourists and full of charm. It's a great place for gelato and a stroll in the late afternoon. The old Roman spa of Bagno Vignoni is just south of town. It's a must-see, and you can even try out one of the modern spas near the Roman bath. Market day is the first and fourth Tuesday of each month.

Saturnia: On the southern coast of Tuscany, this spa town considers itself the first city in Italy: pre-Etruscan fragments have been discovered in the area, although the design of the present town dates from the Roman era. If you want an adventure, park your car along the road before you reach town (coming from the south) and follow the bathers (and the sulfur smell) down the dirt road to the "public spa." There are no changing rooms, so be prepared! You will meet people from all over the globe splashing and swimming in the hot sulfur water. Ristorante I Due Cippi, in town, may look rather ordinary outside, but the décor is lovely, and the menu is interesting.

Siena: A city within a city, Siena consists of an ancient medieval center ringed by a modern Italian city. Definitely worth a day's exploration, park in one of the structures near the city center and walk into the heart of old Siena. To access the most convenient parking, take the San Marco exit (from the north) or the Est exit (from the south) off the superstrada, following the signs for Siena Parcheggio Duomo (a blue "P" sign). For specialty food shops, try: Vini e Vizi - La Bottega di Andrea (Via Montanani 9, on the main street) and Consorzio Agrario Provinciale di Siena (Via Pianciani, near the post office). An excellent restaurant is Al Marsili, located in a beautifully decorated room with brick alcoves. In season, they serve fantastic grilled porcini mushrooms (3 Via del Castoro; Tel. (+39) 0577 47154). The best place to taste and buy regional wine is the government-sponsored Enoteca Italiana di Siena (Piazza Matteotti 30; open 4PM–12AM). Market day is Wednesday.

Siena really comes alive around the time of its famous no-holds-barred horse race, the Palio (July 2 and August 16). This medieval horse race is truly an event to experience, and it's worth the expense to purchase good seats, but only if you plan about a year in advance (otherwise it will be completely sold out). For a list of merchants or organizations that sell tickets, contact the Azienda Autonoma di Turismo (Piazza del Campo 56, 53100 Siena; Tel. (+39) 0577 280551; Fax (+39) 0577 270676 or (+39) 0577 281041).

Southern Tuscan Coast: If you're after the Italian beach life but want to avoid the crowds, head down the southern coast (but not in August!) to Ansedonia, Orbetello, and Monte Argentario. Not much is left of ancient Ansedonia, although up a steep hill you can find Roman ruins of the old city of Cosa. Today, Ansedonia is composed of a small hotel with a restaurant and hillsides of secluded villas overlooking the sea. Orbetello is charming, with good places to eat and a nice downtown area closed off to cars. It's an agreeable spot for an evening *passeggiata* (stroll). Continuing on the causeway from Orbetello to Monte Argentario, you can go south to the resort town of Porto Ercole or north to Porto Santo Stefano. Both are elegant beach resorts. The delightful village of Capalbio is located just six kilometers inland and is an easy drive for lunch or dinner or a stroll up its winding streets.

Vinci: The birthplace of Leonardo da Vinci, this lovely little town sits west of Florence, surrounded by hills of olives and grapevines. You'll find a fascinating museum filled with the drawings and accompanying models of Leonardo's inventions, all with English descriptions next to the Itaian. The museum is definitely worth a visit for both children and adults.

Volterra: This regional gem truly captures the "hill town experience" in full. From the characteristic main piazza to its Roman ruins, Volterra has something from every century all the way back to Etruscan times. Wander along Etruscan walls dating from the 4th century BC or purchase your own alabaster memento in a nearby shop. Visit museums, the exterior of a 15th century fortress, or lounge in the Piazza dei Priori, one of the best town squares in the region-- and the site of many historic and often bloody events.

UMBRIA

Known as the Green Heart of Italy, Umbria is characterized by verdant rolling hills, fields of yellow sunflowers, the smoky flavor of truffles, and the tang of sheep's milk cheese. It is both refined and wild. A land of Etruscan and medieval origins, Umbria is steeped in spirituality: the hill town of Assisi, birthplace of St. Francis, is the center of the Franciscan monastic movement. Perugia, Umbria's capital, hosts a world famous jazz festival, while Gubbio puts on an annual pagan celebration. Spoleto, Orvieto, and Urbino are also gems of the region. Perugia, home to Perugina chocolates, has an international chocolate festival each fall. Perugia's other delicacies include the delectable umbricelli pasta (a specialty of Northern Umbria), bruschetta, farro soup, pork dishes, wild pigeon, and squab. As for truffles, dogs or pigs sniff out these precious mushrooms in the area around Norcia and Spoleto. The cuisine of Southern Umbria highlights the subtle combination of truffles, olive oil, cheese, and homemade pasta. The white wine of Orvieto is the region's most famous. Enjoy!

ACTIVITIES:

Tours and Cooking Classes: Anne of "Anne's Italy" is an American woman who has lived in Umbria for years. She will introduce you to the land she has come to love through tours of various towns as well as her cooking classes. Website: www.annesitaly.com

PLACES:

Assisi: Everyone seems to know about Assisi, and the droves of tour buses attest to that fact. It's a site of religious pilgrimage for many, as this is the birthplace of both Saint Francis and Saint Clare. It's worth a visit to see the frescos by Giotto, which were restored after the earthquakes in 1997. They are located in the Basilica of San Francesco. The town is particularly lovely in the evening, after the "day-trippers" go home! Market day is Saturday.

Deruta: A charming small town with parking outside the gates, Deruta is the place to buy ceramics. You'll probably lose your mind trying to decide which shop has the best selection! The most well-known shop is U. Grazia on Via Tiberina 181. While you're trying to make up your mind about what to buy, stop at Fontannina for lunch. It has a nice outside patio with a large tree for shade and a beautiful view of the valley (V. Solitaria 14/A/1; Tel: (+39) 075 9724033). Market day is Tuesday.

Gubbio: As you approach this truly spectacular town, you'll be struck by the sight of parallel rows of stone buildings built into the hillside. The view from the beautiful Piazza della Signoria is breathtaking. Gubbio is the town (along with Deruta) in which to purchase hand-painted ceramics from shops that line the Via dei Consoli, the main street. For a gourmet lunch, head to Fornace di Mastro Giorgio on the street of the same name (Tel. 075 922 1836; closed Tuesday). Another good restaurant recommended by clients is Taverna del Lupo on Via Ansidei. Markets held on the second weekend of the month.

Orvieto: Midway between Florence and Rome, Orvieto is a picturesque town perched on a pedestal of volcanic tufa (compressed rock) rising 900 feet above the valley floor. If you follow the signs to Campo la Fiera (look for the blue parking symbol) you'll arrive at a parking structure where you can then take the escalator to the top. Orvieto's cathedral, one of Italy's greatest, is a must-see. Another fascinating structure is the Pozzo di San Patrizio, or Well of Saint Patrick, dating from 1527. A "double helix" staircase allows you to walk 200 feet down into the well and back up again without retracing your steps. The town is surrounded by fantastic landscapes of fields and vineyards. We recommend La Grotta del Funaro, a restaurant tucked in the corner of the tufa rock at the edge of town. Start your meal with the *antipasti misti*, a wonderful assortment of salads, olives, marinated eggplant, artichoke hearts, and roasted peppers (Via Ripa Serancia 41; Tel. (+39) 0763 343276; closed Mondays). Market day is Thursday.

Perugia: As Florence is special to Tuscany, Perugia is the Umbrian jewel. It's very cosmopolitan, filled with ancient treasures-- a wonderful city to explore on foot. The evening passeggiata, when everyone descends upon the main square to stroll and be seen, is a lively spectacle. Head for the underground parking and take the escalators up to the main piazza. For the jazz lover, the well-known Umbria Jazz Festival takes place in July. For more information, go to **www.umbriajazz.com**. Markets held the last weekend of the month.

Rocca Ripesena: This is a small town at the base of Mount Peglia, near Orvieto. This rural area is scattered with volcanic stone and ancient Etruscan ruins, and there are many hiking trails through the scenic natural landscape. (Dedicated hikers may want to take an afternoon and go all the way to Orvieto!) Many of the small medieval villages and towns in the area are inhabited by artists who continue to produce traditional handicrafts.

Spello: Southeast of Assisi, Spello is its smaller and more intimate twin. It's a charming little town with winding streets and lovely vistas. It also has a restaurant, Il Molino, which serves delicious grilled meats, bruschetta, and porcini when in season. (Piazza Matteotti 6/7; Tel. (+39) 0742 651305; closed Tuesdays.) Market day is Wednesday.

Spoleto: A charming town at any time, Spoleto livens up during the Festivale dei Due Mondi, a music festival held every summer from mid-June to mid-July. The local cuisine is delicious: this is where you should eat truffles! For information on the festival, call (800) 56 56 00 (toll-free from within Italy) or (+39) 0743 44700. You can also email **boxoffice@spoletofestival.it**. Market day is Friday.

Todi: Another pretty hill town, Todi is filled with narrow, winding streets and stairs. It also has beautiful vistas of the surrounding countryside. For wonderful food in an awe-inspiring setting, go to L'Umbria and ask to sit on the terrace (under the arches off the Piazza del Popolo; Tel. (+39) 075 894 2737).

Torgiano: This medieval hill town still has its ancient walls and a tower. Low hills covered with vineyards and olives surround the area. In the town center are the Church of S. Maria nel Castello and the Church of the Madonna dell'Ulivello, with paintings from the 16th and 17th centuries. There are also wine and olive oil museums at the palazzo of Graziani-Baglioni. Tre Vaselle is the best restaurant in the area.

CINQUE TERRE (& ITALIAN RIVIERA)

The five charming villages that make up the Cinque Terre are no longer undiscovered. Nevertheless, you are sure to fall in love with the towns, the food, the hikes, and the views. It's wonderful to hike along the narrow trails that connect the five towns of Monterosso, Vernazza, Manarola, Corniglia, and Riomaggiore. Each town offers the opportunity to enjoy the local cuisine and wine. Bring comfortable shoes with good tread, as the trails can be slippery in drizzle.

The broader area of Liguria, including the Italian Riviera, also encompasses Portofino and Rapallo, two small coastal towns east of Genoa. These are lovely, ritzy spots known for attracting the "jet set." On the southern end of Liguria, Portovenere and Lerici are very charming towns. In fact, Portovenere is a great base for exploring the Cinque Terre by ferry.

ACTIVITIES:

Hiking: The *sentieri* are the hiking paths that connect the Cinque Terre and the two towns of Levanto (north of Monterosso) and Portovenere (south of Rio Maggiore). Some of the paths are steep and long, and others are short and fairly level. If you pack a lunch, you will have a perfect day's outing walking from one town to another. Keep in mind that there is now a charge of a few Euros for using these trails; if you will also be using the train, you can buy a one-day pass at the train station that covers all costs.

Train/Ferry: It is possible to see the Cinque Terre by a combination of train, ferry travel, and hiking. Timetables are variable, particularly for ferries, so plan on consulting a schedule when you arrive.

Eating Out: Finding interesting restaurants or *trattorie* in the Cinque Terre is easy, particularly if you like seafood and pesto. Be sure to try the fresh anchovies with lemon! This is also the area famous for focaccia, so be sure to have several samples.

PLACES:

Corniglia: This Cinque Terre town is distinct because it is the only town not directly beside the sea. Instead, it sits about 100 meters above sea level. The town is reached via the *Lardarina*, a path of 377 steps. The village has a view of the other four Cinque Terre towns.

Genoa: Purported birthplace of Christopher Columbus, this city has recently experienced a revival in popularity. UNESCO has added Genoa to its list of World Heritage Sites because of its numerous palazzi. There is also a cathedral, the second-largest aquarium in the world, and an opera house. Genoa's most famous landmark is its medieval gates, flanked by two crenellated towers. Markets held on the first Saturday of the month (except Aug. and Sept.) at Palazzo Ducale.

Manarola: Probably the oldest of the Cinque Terre towns, Manarola has its own dialect. The Via dell'Amore (road of love) hiking trail runs between Manarola and Riomaggiore, and is an easy walk or stroll.

Monterosso al Mare: This Cinque Terre town has the only sizeable sand beach on the coast. You can also visit a partially-ruined castle and the Parish church of St. John the Baptist.

Portofino: This small Italian fishing village is known as one of the most beautiful Mediterranean ports. Once frequented by Richard Burton, Elizabeth Taylor, and Rex Harrison, today Portofino is host to many upscale vacation residences as well as a ring of restaurants and cafés on the waterfront.

Portovenere: The characteristic medieval town of Portovenere has many sights to offer, including the Genoese Castle, the Church of St. Pietro on the cliffs, Byron's Grotto, San Lorenzo Church, and the narrow, high, many- colored houses. Stop and admire the view of Poet's Gulf, Palmaria Island, Lerici, and Tellaro. This is the perfect jumping-off place for visiting the Cinque Terre.

Rapallo: In this seaside town you will find fancy yachts anchored in the bay and casual seafood restaurants alongside designer shops. The bay is also notable for the presence of the rather unique castle, built right on the water at the end of a small rocky jetty, originally to protect the town from pirate raids. In Rapallo there are also several interesting churches and public buildings to visit. Market day is Thursday.

Riomaggiore: Dating from the 13th century, this Cinque Terre town is known for its wine. It is the southernmost of the five towns.

Vernazza: This Cinque Terre town is entirely pedestrian and has managed to maintain its "fishing village" feel. Market day is Tuesday.

DETAILS:

Arriving: The best way to visit the Cinque Terre is by ferry, train, and hiking. It makes sense to access the towns from Portovenere, Levanto, or La Spezia. Portovenere offers easy access by ferry, while Levanto and La Spezia are on the same train line as the five Cinque Terre towns, with trains running all day.

ITALIAN LAKES

Located at the foot of the Alps, the Italian Lakes (Como, Maggiore, Garda, and Orta) are the jewels of northern Italy. They are spread across three regions: Lombardy, Verona, and Piedmont. Surrounded by quaint towns such as Como, Tremezzo, and Bellagio and lined with patrician villas, the lakes offer countless opportunities for exploration. While a trip by ferry is an ideal way to take in the views, there are many hiking trails that afford even more panoramic vistas. In the unlikely event that you tire of blue sky and even bluer water, the fashion capital of Milan is nearby, as are Mantova, Brescia, and Cremona. Lombardy is known for its incredible cheese: bel paese, gorgonzola, mascarpone, and taleggio are but a sampling of the region's delights. Other wonderful specialties include bresaola, minestrone, polenta, and risotto.

ACTIVITIES:

Hiking: The Italian Lakes are excellent for all levels of hiking: difficulty increases as you go up! Strollers can keep to the lakeside, while dedicated climbers will want to conquer more strenuous trails and be rewarded with some truly incredible vistas. For trail information, stop into a tourist office (easily located in the main towns). Do make sure to take a map, however, as hikers have been known to get dangerously lost.

Ferries: The most practical way of getting across the lakes, ferries are also a great way to see the landscape. Ferries run fairly frequently, so it's not difficult to catch them without much planning. However, if you can read Italian, you will find official timetables on this website: www.navlaghi.it.

Water Sports: The lakes offer many opportunities for water-based activities. Companies operate along the lakeshore, offering everything from windsurfing to individual boat rentals. Check the local tourist information office for ideas.

Cuisine: You probably won't be surprised to find that lakeside cuisine is based primarily on fish. Specialties include misultitt (fish desiccated in containers called misolte) and soused fish (fried and then pickled), along with more traditional dishes like rice with perch or smoked trout.

PLACES:

Bellagio (on Como): Known as "la perla del lago" (the pearl of the lake), the rural fishing village of Bellagio is considered by many to be the most beautiful town in Europe. Its narrow cobbled streets, breathtaking views, impeccable homes and glorious villas make it an enchanting spot to explore. A beautiful Baroque church highlights the main square, and nearby is a restaurant serving fresh fish. There are several other excellent restaurants, pizzerias, and bars. Boat tours of the lake's villages, villas, and Comacina Island can be reserved in town.

Borromean Islands (on Maggiore): Near Stresa, these four islands have been in the same family since the 12th century. Isola Bella, the largest, is occupied by a villa built by Carlo III Borromeo in honor of his wife Isabella. Isola dei Pescatori harbors an ancient fishing village with tiny narrow streets and some good eating. Isola Madre has another Borromean palace and noteworthy botanical gardens. Finally, Isola di San Giovanni is the smallest, located just off Pallanza.

Como: Located at the southernmost tip of the lake which bears its name, this elegant town is perfect for a day's outing. Sights in town include the Duomo, the austere church of San Abbondio, Villa Carlotta, the Piazza S. Fedele (with many 400-year-old buildings), and the Basilica, one of the masterpieces of the *maestri comacini* (Como masters). Before leaving, be sure to take the funicular up to Brunate, a small village with a spectacular view. Markets held the first Saturday of the month in Piazza San Fedele.

Lake Garda: With its clear, clean, warm water, sunny beaches, mild climate and Mediterranean vegetation, Lake Garda sits like a small sea halfway between Venice and Milan. A favored spot since Roman times, Garda has been lauded by poets and writers throughout the ages, including Goethe, Joyce, and D'Annunzio. It unites natural beauty with historical remains, from Roman ruins onward. Many interesting towns are scattered along the coast and up the hills, like Salo, Gardone Riviera, and the beautiful Sirmione, rich with history, culture, good restaurants, and shops. You'll also find opportunities and facilities for almost any type of sport or activity you can think of: windsurfing, sailing, golf, rock-climbing, and even bungee jumping! Accessing sights on the opposite side of the lake is made easy by a half-hour ferry connection from Toscolano Maderno to Torri del Benaco, running every 30 minutes.

Lake Orta: To the west of Lake Maggiore, this small lake offers an escape from the busier scene of the larger Italian Lakes, while offering a variety of water sports, lush vegetation, and many footpaths from villages into the hills and mountains. The primary town of the lake is Orta S.Giulio, where there are a wide range of shops and good restaurants. This charming medieval village has wonderful palaces and lanes that lead to the ancient square facing the lake where the 16th century Palazzotto stands. This is an area rich in Romanesque and Baroque architecture. Isola San Giulio is the only island on Lake Orta, taking its name from a local saint (Julius) who lived in the 4th century. The island is dominated by the Basilica of Saint Giulio.

Menaggio (on Como): Once a walled city, some of the remnants are still visible in Menaggio today. In the summer, this town is a popular recreation area, with opportunities for windsurfing, water skiing, and other water-based activities. You could also rent a bicycle and explore the area or take a walk down the lakeside promenade, lined with flowers. Because of its central location, Menaggio is a great base for exploring the rest of the area. Drive down the lakeshore road to Tremezzo and Como, or hop on a ferry to visit Varenna or Bellagio.

Toscolano Maderno (on Garda): Situated on the western side of Lake Garda, this village has bars, Tabacchi shops, and the delicious Trattoria San Carlo. Sights to see include the 12th century church of S. Andrea and its Parish (with work by Paolo Veneziano and Paolo Veronese), the Valle delle Cartiere (where the paper-making industry once flourished), the 16th century church of Santi Pietro e Paolo (with sculptures and paintings), and the Sanctuary of the Madonna del Benaco (with 16th century frescoes).

DETAILS:

Arriving: Unless you're driving in from another part of Italy, odds are that you'll be flying into the Milan-Malpensa airport. Do be aware that the airport is about 50 km outside of the city of Milan, so you will need to prepare in advance if you won't be going to your property directly after you land. See Chapter Two for information about flying into Milan.

Driving: Although there are many towns around the Italian lakes, you are probably better off renting a car than depending strictly on public transportation. Many of the villas and accommodations available on the lakes are spread out between the towns, and it is particularly handy (not to mention pleasant) to drive around the lakefront road whenever you want.

VENETO

The Veneto truly caters to all travelers' tastes. There are mountains (the Dolomites), lakes (Garda), beaches (the Adriatic), and monumental cultural centers (Venice, Verona, Vicenza, and Padova). The region offers an extraordinary range of scenery and remains one of the richest in Italy. Although the canals of Venice steal the show, the nightly summertime operas in Verona's Roman forum are beyond compare. To the northeast lies the Friuli region, home of some of the world's finest white wines, and historic towns such as Udine and Trieste. There are also many other wonderful towns in the area that are less well-known and less frequented by tourists. *Italian Neighbors*, by Tim Parks, is a fun book written by an Englishman who moved to a small town outside of Verona. It provides a good introduction to the joys and struggles of life as a foreigner in the Veneto region.

ACTIVITIES:

Cultural Calendar: For current, up-to-date information about Veneto's cultural events, visit the region's official website at **www.veneto.to**.

Opera: For the opera schedule in Verona, visit **www.verona.com/arena**

PLACES:

Asolo: If you drive to the pretty town of Asolo, also be sure to visit (or at least drive through) Castelfranco Veneto, Cittadella, and Bassano del Grappa. Asolo is perched on a hill and is every bit as picturesque as the books say it is. For lunch, go to the Hosteria Ca' Derton (Piazza D'Annunzio 11; Tel. (+39) 042 352 9648). If porcini is in season, order the *porcini alla griglia con polenta* (grilled mushrooms with polenta). A memorable dish! Markets held the first Saturday and second Sunday of each month (except July and August).

Lake Garda: For a spectacular drive, take the road around the lake, beginning at the north end. You'll be amazed at the changes in the landscape and the character of the towns as you drive from north to south. The east side of the lake is said to be slower-paced and less expensive than the west side.

Marostica: This is the town of the human chess game (*Partita a Scacchi*) that is staged every two years (even numbered years in September) in the main piazza. Marostica is a charming medieval town, complete with old walls and a castle atop the hill (worth a hike for the views). A great place for lunch is the Pizzeria-Trattoria All'Alfiere (Piazza Castello 16, on the main piazza). If you're there on Sunday, be sure to visit the museum in the castle on the square, where costumes used in the chess match are on display. For information about attending the event, visit www.marosticascacchi.it. Markets held the first Sunday of the month in Piazza Castello.

Vicenza: Like Verona, a part of old Vicenza is blocked off to automobile traffic. Home of Palladio, the famous High Renaissance architect, the city is full of his designs. With your guidebook in hand, walk through the Piazza Signori, across the Ponte San Marco, and then back to the Teatro Olimpico. The old town is small, intimate, and alive with Italians. For lunch or dinner, try Tre Visi; the food is delicious and the ambiance pleasing (Contra Porti 6, Tel. (+39) 044 432 4868). Market day is Thursday in the Piazza dei Signori.

Verona: The city of *Romeo and Giulietta* is graceful, elegant, and sophisticated. The best way to approach the city is to go through the Porta Nuova and then find a parking place (there is a large parking garage on the right that is quite close to the Piazza Bra). The ancient Arena, which dominates the Piazza Bra, is the scene of innumerable concerts and operas throughout the year. It is worthwhile to pay the admission fee and explore the inside, climbing to the top for a view of the piazza. From there you should walk down the Via Mazzini to the Piazza Erbe, another beautiful piazza, and explore medieval Verona. The summer opera season at the Arena runs July through August. For information about the opera season, visit www.verona.com (in Italian) or www.arena.it (English or Italian). For an expensive treat, stop at

Dodici Apostoli, near the Piazza Erbe. This restaurant is rather hard to find, since it's located on a tiny square, but the search is worthwhile. The interior features a traditional Renaissance setting with frescoed walls (Corticella San Marco 3, Tel. 045 596 6999). Markets held the third Sunday of the month in Piazza San Zeno.

AMALFI COAST

Because of its precarious position on the steep coastal cliffs, the Amalfi Coast can only be reached by a long, winding drive. Once you exit the tunnel at Castelnuovo, however, you will enter an enchanted world of gleaming blue water and lemon-scented air. The Amalfi Coast includes Sorrento and the islands of Ischia and Capri. You'll quickly become aware of the "organized chaos" that governs life in southern Italy. On the Amalfi Coast, as anywhere in Italy, you must go with the flow, whether in your car, on the streets, or at the beaches. And here, perhaps more than anywhere else, that flow is often slowed to a snail's pace. So relax... enjoy it!

ACTIVITIES:

Dining: The seafood and produce in Campania (the larger region including the Amalfi coast) is out of this world. The cuisine is fresh, inventive, and zippy. Be sure to order the *insalata caprese*, a regional specialty. The local produce sold at stands along the roadside is a good indication of ingredients to look for when selecting from a menu: lemons, cherry tomatoes, garlic, and peperoncini. Another regional specialty is limoncello, a slightly sweet *digestivo* that tastes sharply of lemon rind and is served ice cold. You'll find it everywhere. As for restaurants, here are a couple of suggestions in Positano: Ristorante le Tre Sorelle (Via del Brigantino 23/25; Tel. (+39) 089 811461); Ristorante Chez Black (Via del Briagantino 19; Tel. (+39) 089 875036); and Buca di Bacco (Via Rampa Teglia 4; Tel. (+39) 089 875699).

Hiking: It will become immediately obvious upon your arrival on the Amalfi Coast that steps are unavoidable-- just living there qualifies as exercise. However, if you are a dedicated hiker you may want to tackle some of the local trails. Check out www.amalficoastweb.com for some hiking maps.

Nightlife: Whether you're in the mood for a cocktail or want to dance the night away Euro-style, here's a spot to try in Positano: Music on the Rocks (Grotte dell'Incanto 51; Tel. (+39) 089 875874).

Swimming: Depending on your budget, taking a dip in the sea can be prohibitively expensive. In order to access the beach you have to purchase the use of a chair and an umbrella from a bathing establishment, which will cost you upwards of 10 Euros. So, where to go when you just want to cool off? A local directed us to the following spot: Departing Amalfi towards Positano, look for a sign on the right that says "Grotto degli Artisti." Just beyond the sign, you'll see a banner for a windsurfing school. Directly opposite (on the west side of the road) you'll see an opening in the fence. Proceed through this opening and down the 500 or so steps (it's not as bad as it sounds). On the beach, you'll see the windsurfing school; their property is clearly marked. The rest is all yours! It's not a place where you'd want to spend the whole day, but it is a great place to get wet, cool off, and get a little exercise, thanks to the stairs!

PLACES:

Amalfi: An important trading center from the 9th to 13th centuries, Amalfi is surrounded by striking cliffs and coast. Among many shops and cafes you will enjoy the lovely architecture that surrounds you, including the Duomo in the center of town and the Cloister of Paradise, which takes a cue from Arabian styles. There is also a museum dedicated to the works of Morelli and a museum where you can view artifacts of Amalfi's long and interesting history. Of course, don't forget to spend some time on the beach! Amalfi is also a great starting place for exploring the rest of the coast, as the central bus yard is located down by the water, along with ferries and a handy tourist information shop. Market day is Wednesday on Via Fiume.

Atrani: Notable as the smallest town in Italy and pictured in one of M. C. Escher's lithographs, Atrani seems to hang right on the edge of the sea. It is an incredibly magical, picturesque spot and well worth any time spent here.

Capri: Beyond the hype, Capri more than lives up to its reputation as a truly exquisite, elegant island. It has its fair share of prestigious boutiques (you'll find every purveyor of luxury goods under the sun) but there's also a pristine, earthy quality that you sense as you meander through the streets and peek into residents' gardens. It's a vacation hot spot, but it's also a living island that still belongs to the natives—not just to the beautiful people who flock here. Once you arrive at the harbor, you must take the funicular up to the town of Capri. Be warned, however, visiting on the weekends or during July and August can be suffocating because of the sheer volume of tourists. Once in Capri, you have lots of options, all of which are wonderful.

Hint: If you're visiting Capri for the day, don't leave home without a bathing suit, so you can visit this otherworldly place for a dip: As you exit the funicular, head west on Via Faraglion and climb the steps to the square, then proceed directly through town on the main road. Stay on this road until you see a paved path leading down towards the water. Follow the path. It turns into stairs, and it's indeed quite a hike, but once you glimpse the majestic Faraglioni in the distance, it's all worth it. The swimming spot boasts some of the clearest, bluest water you'll see on the coast. For a charge you can swim, store your things in a locker, and grab a cold shower. For an additional cost you can also rent a beach chair and spend the afternoon. There is also a small restaurant.

Maiori: Sitting in the deepest inlet of the Amalfi coast, at the mouth of a river, Maiori boasts the largest beach on the Amalfi Coast. During the middle ages, Maiori was the primary harbor of the Amalfi Republic, housing arsenals and military headquarters. It was surrounded by coastal fortifications, some of which remain today. Along with remains of towers you can still see the Castle of San Francesco, built in the 15th century. Sights in town include the Santa Maria a Mare, a domed 12th century church in the center of town, the Church of St Nicola de Thoro-Plano, the Castle of St Nicola, the monastic complex of St Maria de Olearia, and the sanctuary of St Maria delle Grazie. Market day is Friday on Corso Regina.

Naples: Though not the most attractive city on the surface, Naples has a long and interesting history. We recommend exploring it with a guide who can direct you to the things you want to see and steer you away from the less savory parts of town. Context Travel offers a unique way to see Naples, walking through the city with an architect, historian, or art expert. **www.contexttravel.com**

Positano: No doubt about it; Positano is one of the most picturesque towns in the world. Teetering on the edge of a cliff, it looks like a layered wedding cake. Once prosperous in the 16th and 17th centuries, Positano had fallen on hard times by the 1800's; many of the inhabitants emigrated to the US, and Positano became just another "poor fishing village." But it was a fishing village filled with charm, and when John Steinbeck visited in the 1950's he wrote: "Positano bites deep. It is a dream place that isn't quite real when you are there and becomes beckoningly real after you have gone." Others agreed, and today Positano is once again a glittering jewel of the Mediterranean. Positano is also well known for its clothing boutiques. By car you enter the town from one direction and exit from the other. There are garages lining the road into town, but the closer you get to the center, the more expensive the garage fees. Do note that Positano is a city of stairs! You must be in good physical condition to handle the constant up and down.

Ravello: High above the Amalfi Coast, this elegant and aristocratic town sits on a 350 foot rocky spur, reached only by an impossibly narrow road with hair-raising turns. Offering magnificent palazzos, churches, and gardens bearing witness to its noble history, Ravello's rich cultural life complements an unmatched, striking beauty. One of the most important monuments is the Cathedral, founded in 1086, but there is also the church of San Giovanni del Toro, the churches of Santa Maria a Gradillo and Santissima Annunziata, Villa Episcopio, and the Piazza Fontana Moresca. Don't miss the opportunity to stroll in the gardens of Villa Cimerona or Villa Rufolo. Both estates boast carefully maintained classical Italian gardens, sculptures, and incredible lookouts over the sea and surrounding coastline. Villa Rufolo is situated just beyond the main square, while Villa Cimerona is slightly further; just follow the signs. Ravello is famous for its summer classical music concerts, held at Villa Rufolo. Tickets can be purchased in advance through the Ravello Concert Society: **www.ravelloarts.org**. Market day is Tuesday.

Sorrento: Larger than the tiny Amalfi Coast towns, Sorrento is a bustling city with hotels on either end. The old center of town is closed to traffic and full of restaurants and fascinating shops. Going into the heart of Sorrento, you'll find yourself in a thriving seaside community, filled with life, good food, and great shopping. Sorrento is a great place to buy coral, and is likewise famous for two things you can't miss: limoncello (an alcoholic aperitif) and inlaid wood. The workshops of Sorrento were the first to use the technique of arranging small pieces of wood into intricate patterns, a practice which has been refined and perfected through generations. There are also a couple of places you ought not to miss. The first is the 10th century Basilica di San Antonio. Saint Anthony is the patron of navigators, and sailors have made thousands of votive offerings at his tomb in the crypt. The 11th century Cathedral is also beautiful, housing some frescoes and a bell tower with a ceramic clock. The cloisters of Saint Francis are interesting because they have been "restored" many times over the centuries, resulting in an array of architectural styles from late gothic to the renaissance. The Sorrento Summer of Music series is held at the cloisters every year from July to September, featuring international musicians performing alongside of emerging musical talents. The Circumvesuviana train goes from Naples to Sorrento, with several stops along the way at such places as Ercolano (Herculaneum) and Pompeii. The bus station is located near the train station. In addition, the port is close by, with frequent hydrofoils and ferries to Naples, Capri, Ischia, and Positano. Market day is Tuesday on Via Sant'Antonio.

DETAILS:

Arriving: There are several ways to get to the Amalfi Coast. The best way is simply to hire a driver to pick you up in Naples (either at the airport or train station) and take you to your destination. There are less expensive ways to arrive, but a driver avoids most of the hassle and will get you there quickly. You can also follow the autostrada in from Rome, rent a car in Naples, or take the Circumvesuviana train from Naples to Sorroento and then hop on a bus or hydrofoil to your final destination.

Circumvesuviana: This convenient train runs about every half hour between the Naples train station and Sorrento, making stops in Ercolano (Herculaneum) and Pompeii. Tickets can be bought directly at the station. A trip from Sorrento to Naples takes about an hour.

Buses: Other than ferries, perhaps the most convenient way to get around the Amalfi Coast is by bus. These enormous vehicles lumber fearlessly around every corner, threading both ways along roads only large enough for one car-- in short, an experience that will leave your heart in your throat! These blue SITA busses cost a few Euros, depending on your destination; you'll need to purchase general tickets ahead of time and then validate them when you get on the bus. Stops are marked with a blue and white SITA sign. General driving times are: Ravello to Amalfi, 15 minutes; Amalfi to Positano, 30 minutes; Positano to Sorrento, 35 minutes. It's a good idea to leave yourself some time in case of traffic jams or other unanticipated delays. For schedules and more information (unfortunately only in Italian), visit www.sitabus.it.

Drivers: Here are some recommended driver services. These companies (and individuals) provide both transfer services and private guided driving tours.

- Persico: **www.persicocarservice.com**
- Nicola Mangieri: Tel. (+39) 089 872881; Car (+39) 336 852566
- Positano: **www.positanocarservice.com**
- Cuomo Limo: **www.cuomonet.it**
- Host 2 Coast: **www.host2cost.com**

Driving: The Amalfi Coast road (163) is potentially treacherous, trafficked by both speedy locals and monstrous tour buses. Use caution at all times, especially around blind turns, and don't be afraid to honk your horn. The buses have the right-of-way, so if you see one bearing down on you, stop and pull over as far as possible to let the bus pass. Be prepared for traffic jams during the summer months, and the smaller your car, the better off you are. Parking is at a premium so you'll often pay astronomical prices. For those with nerves of steel, a scooter offers a convenient alternative. You might notice that cars parking along this road have turned in their mirrors to avoid removal. Frankly, we suggest taking a bus!

Ferries: From late April to mid-October, ferries depart frequently from Amalfi and Positano, going to Capri, Sorrento, Salerno, and Minori. Schedules will vary by season, so stop by a tourist information office for a schedule when you arrive. Taking a ferry is an excellent way to admire the fantastic coastline, and pretty much the only way to see the cliff-side towns as a whole. The best place to catch a ferry is probably in Amalfi, as the English-speaking tourist/transportation office is clearly visible just across the road from the water. There are many different ferry lines, but the Coop Sant'Andrea offers fairly comprehensive services at **www.coopsantandrea.com**. For more private boat rentals, check out **www.lucibello.it**.

Naples: Most people arrive at the Amalfi Coast via Naples. Prepare yourself for the gritty outskirts as you leave-- they are indeed a sobering sight compared to the prosperity in other areas. Consider this portion of your trip an education: Naples has become a kind of international port, with immigrants arriving from Africa and other poor areas, desperate for work.

SICILY

For adventurous travelers who love antiquity, Sicily is an ideal destination. In order to see everything (and there is a lot), be prepared for the traffic and, unfortunately, the litter that are a part of everyday life in any Sicilian city. About 90% of the population resides in an urban center, which means that once you leave any city center you will be struck by the lack of people and cars. As you drive from the desert-like southern coast to the mountainous interior, or from the lush north coast to majestic Mount Etna, you will become aware of the diverse geography of the island. In the following pages are some ideas and places that simply shouldn't be missed-- and a few places to avoid.

ACTIVITIES:

Food and Wine: Arancini are pear-size balls of rice wrapped around cheese or meat sauce and fried in oil-- don't miss this Sicilian specialty! Try them for a mid-day snack or even a whole lunch. Consider stopping by one of the many small wineries you will pass as you drive through the countryside. Signs read "Vino 3 Euros." Ask for a brief tour of the wine cellar (cava). Though wines are of varying quality, wineries offer a chance to experience warm Sicilian hospitality.

Mount Etna: This fascinating active volcano has the longest period of documented eruptions in the world, and any visit to Sicily should involve at least some time spent around this natural wonder. Etna offers skiing in the winter and breathtaking woodland hikes throughout the summer.

Ceramics: As in much of Italy, terra cotta ceramics are a traditional handicraft. Traditional Sicilian terra cotta features intricate designs inspired by Moorish and Baroque styles. The best areas to buy ceramics are Caltagirone, Monreale, and Santo Stefano di Camastra.

PLACES:

Southern Sicily: It's possible to visit the spectacular Valle dei Templi without driving into modern Agrigento. The temples are not to be missed. It is also possible to see the old town of Ortygia, the *citta vecchia* (old city) of Syracuse without driving through the modern city. Unfortunately, to reach the archeological zone it is necessary to drive through a portion of the modern city. Still, it's manageable. The Greco-Roman and Palaeo-Christian ruins are fascinating. The Baroque city of Noto, near Syracuse, is absolutely worth a stop. Another nice town in the same area is Ragusa Ibla, the old town of Ragusa. You won't find many tourists in these two towns, but you will find charm and good food!

Further afield from Agrigento are two other archeological sites with exceptional Greek ruins: Selinunte and Segesta. Just north of Gela (truly an ugly city, but home to an important archeological museum) is Piazza Amerina, where the Villa Romana del Casale is located about 4 km southwest of town. The villa itself, as well as the spectacular mosaic floors, will delight all ages. A very interesting and worthwhile side trip about twenty minutes from the Villa Romana is the Scavi di Morgantina (excavations of Morgantina), a pre-Hellenistic city destroyed by the Romans. You won't find many tourists in this lovely spot, and there are lots of ruins to explore.

Northern Sicily: The charming fishing village/resort of Cefalu is a pleasant base for exploring this part of Sicily. Cefalu remains a truly Sicilian town, contrasted with Taormina, which has become more of a tourist destination. From Cefalu, it is possible to take side trips to Enna, Mount Etna, Taormina, Monreale, and even Palermo. Taormina is a beautiful place, filled with luxury hotels, tastefully tucked away along picturesque winding streets or jutting out over the sea. The shops are filled with the ceramics of Sicily and bougainvillea cascades down the steep hillsides. Its Greek Theatre has a spectacular setting above the town, overlooking the sea. The *passeggiata*, where everyone in town fills the streets in the early evening to walk, talk, and be seen is a real occasion in Taormina. It should be said, though, that virtually everyone is a tourist or connected with tourism, including the

Italians! Market day in Cefalu is Saturday; Wednesday in Taormina (Via Guardiola Vecchia).

Eastern Sicily: The three fishing villages north of Catania make an enjoyable visit: Acitrezza, home of the great Italian novelist, Verga; Acicastello, where you should hike to the top for magnificent views; and Acireale, where you can stroll down the main street and stop at one of the many restaurants for lunch. Also, take one of the loveliest drives on the island, along highway 185. The town of Novara di Sicilia is particularly enchanting. The highway winds up and down over mountains and through villages. Starting from the north, you will end up in the valley just north of Mount Etna and back onto the A18. If you've rented a property within 50 km of Etna, be prepared to find your vehicle dusted with the fine volcanic ash that falls from Etna after a particularly "active" day.

DETAILS:

Arrival: The easiest way to get to Sicily is by air. The two international airports are Punta Raisi, outside of Palermo, and Fontanarossa, just south of Catania. Of the two airports, Fontanarossa is larger, more modern, and easier to access. It's easy to pick up a rental car from either airport.

Driving: Driving in Sicilian cities is an exercise in courage and patience! Frankly, it's easier to stay out of the cities as much as possible (or at least use public transportation when available). The system of *autostrade* that crisscrosses the island is excellent, and once you leave the outskirts of the main towns and cities, you will encounter very little traffic. Driving conditions are relatively similar to those found on the peninsula, but be prepared to find Sicilians making a 4-lane road out of 2 around rush hour. Stay to the left and keep your eyes on the road.

NOTES:

NOTES:

APPENDIX A:
USEFUL VOCABULARY

English	Italian
Do you speak English?	Parla inglese?
Where is the bathroom?	Dove è il toilette?
What is the cost?	Quanto costa?
Do you accept credit cards?	Accettate carte di credito?
I'd like to go to... [place]	Mi piace andare a...
I'd like to have... [food]	Vorrei un/una...
I am looking for...	Sto cercando...
It's an emergency	È un'emergenza
I don't understand	Non capisco
Bus stop	Fermata del pullman
Train station	La Stazione
Tourist info office	Ufficio informazione (i)
The check	Il conto
Internet café	Cybercafé
ATM	Bancomat
Grocery store	Negozio alimentari
Market	Mercato
Gasoline/Diesel	Benzina/Gasolio
Ticket	Biglietto
Hospital/Emergency Room	Ospedale (H)/Pronto soccorso

APPENDIX B:
METRIC CONVERSIONS

Italy, like most European countries, uses the metric system. Here are the main conversions:

Distances

1.6 km (1,600 metri)	1 mile
0.9 metri	1 yard
30 centimetri (cm)	1 foot
2.5 centimetri	1 inch

Weight

30 gr	1 ounce
455 gr	1 pound
1 chilogrammo (10 etti)	2.2 pounds
1 etto/etti (100 grams)	3.5 ounces

Volume

5 millilitri (ml)	1 teaspoon
15 ml	1 tablespoon
240 ml	1 cup
3.8 litri	1 gallon

INDEX

ATM	47
banks	47
beds	49
buses	25
calling	33
car insurance	10
car rental	9
cell phones	11
children	8
churches	48
coffee makers	50
cook services	7
credit cards	13, 47
currency exchange	47
driving	26
emergency numbers	49
etiquette and attitude	43
gas	27
greetings	44
grocery shopping	33
heating/cooling	45
insurance	7
int'l driving permit	9
internet	11
Italian cuisine	36
Italian life	47
Italian recipes	37
key holder	33, 43
laptop	11
laundry	50
mail	48
metric conversions	115
money	33, 47
mosquitoes	44
museums	8, 47
national holidays	48
packing checklist	16
passports	9
plumbing and electricity	46
rental voucher	9, 13
restrooms	49
road signs	29
safety	49
shopping list	35
strikes	48
tours	7
trains	24
trash and recycling	43
traveler's checks	47
travel supplies	12
useful vocabulary	114
weather	13

Made in the USA
Lexington, KY
16 April 2010